DAVE MATTHEWS SO

MW01015159

CONTENTS

Transcribed by Jeff Jacobson

Album Art Direction & Design: Thane Kerner
Photography: Barnaby Draper

Cherry Lane Music Company
Director of Publications/Project Editor: Mark Phillips
Manager of Publications: Rebecca Quigley

ISBN 1-57560-721-2

Visit our website at www.cherrylane.com

DAVE MATTHEWS SOME DEVIL

Dave Matthews has always done things his own way. In the ten years since the release of the Dave Matthews Band debut, *Remember Two Things*—one of the few independent recordings to sell more than a million copies—DMB have galvanized a community of music fans, releasing multi-platinum live and studio discs year after year. A charismatic and outspoken front man and songwriter, Dave Matthews has stretched the boundaries of rock and pop, integrating jazz, classical, and world music influences with the lyrics of a natural-born storyteller.

It should come as no surprise, then, that when the guitarist/vocalist decided to release his first solo CD, *Some Devil*, there would be a bit of madness to his method. In 2001, Matthews became a first-time father. For a performer who did it his way then hit the highway, becoming the top-grossing touring band of 2000, the change was dramatic. Soon, a new, more personal sound was pouring out of him.

"I have some sort of allegiance to simple melodies, but I was trying to be as experimental as I could be," says Matthews of the experience of writing and recording the songs that would become his solo debut album. On *Some Devil's* lead single, "Gravedigger," he satisfies both urges in two versions—one hauntingly acoustic with orchestrated strings and one as hard-rocking as classic Neil Young.

By turns lush and spare, *Some Devil* offers 13 new compositions by Dave Matthews that range from the stripped-down testimony "of a guilty man who sinned his way to the bottom of the barrel" to lavishly orchestrated, wistful romantic ballads. Though it began as a chance to document songs that, Matthews explains, "hadn't really floated to the surface with the band," *Some Devil* quickly became an ambitious undertaking.

Opening himself up to a self-motivated organic writing process that was "real liberating in one way, but in other ways much more responsibility," Matthews teamed with producer Steve Harris, who'd worked on DMB's *Busted Stuff*. To sketch out the tunes, the pair brought in drummer Brady Blade and bassist Tony Hall who form the rhythm section of Emmylou Harris's band.

"Once there was a rhythm section and things started sounding pretty stomping," Dave recalls, "then the music was really just starting to say to me, well, what else do we need to do?"

The answers arrived along with a group of talented guest musicians. Among them: guitarist Tim Reynolds, who has played for Dave Matthews Band recordings and concerts and toured in acoustic shows with Matthews; Phish guitarist Trey Anastasio, string and horn arranger Audrey Riley, who has worked with Smashing Pumpkins and Coldplay and organist Alex Veley. Together, they and Matthews explored a wealth of styles—from hymnal ("Trouble") to reggae ("Up and Away"), honky-tonk gospel ("Save Me") to the Qawwali devotional groove of Nusfrat Fateh Ali Khan ("An' Another Thing").

Some Devil also provided an opportunity for Matthews to mix it up as a performer. On the folk lullaby "Baby," he recorded live with the Seattlemusic string quartet. For the CD's bluesy title track, Matthews played one-man-band, playing a solitary electric guitar melody echoed in a gritty-to-pretty vocal sweep. Beloved for the way his tough growl and sweet falsetto underscore his complex phrasing and delivery, Matthews unleashes powerful vocal performances that illuminate the passion and pathos of the characters that populate his songs.

Tackling the big themes—life, death, love, loss, and faith—*Some Devil* is filled with songs that explore music's capacity to evoke a multitude of emotions simultaneously. "So Damn Lucky" captures the last thoughts of a man as his car is swerving off the road. The music, says Matthews, is "something that's familiar and painful, full of joy and sad at the same time."

"These songs came out of me with a great deal of honesty. I didn't try to hide behind ambiguity as much as I often think I do. Maybe the fact that I have kids now has made me think that I don't have any more time to be unclear," Matthews explains. "This is the first collection of songs that I've written since my daughters were born and I'm not surprised by the fact that I would more directly deal with mortality."

In doing so, *Some Devil* achieves a delicate balance of dark and light, melancholy and sweetness. "I feel that I'm in a better place than I've ever been in my life and I can only imagine things improving," Matthews says. "Then I came up with this album which has elements of loss and vulnerability."

One thing Dave Matthews has not lost, no matter how much vulnerability his new songs reveal, is a sense of humor about himself. "I think I'm desperately insecure," says the creator of aptly titled *Some Devil*, "but I'm just very comfortable with it."

DODO

Words and Music by
David J. Matthews

6

SO DAMN LUCKY

Words by David J. Matthews
Music by David J. Matthews
and Stephen Harris

Does that scream-ing come from me?

(cont. in slashes)

mf
w/ dist.
w/ slide

Outro

Gtr. 1: w/ Rhy. Fig. 1 (8 times)

E5   Aadd2
Rhy. Fig. 3   End Rhy. Fig. 3

Gtr. 6 tacet

Take me back to just be-fore I was

Riff C   End Riff C

Gtr. 7 (elec.)

mp
w/ dist.

Gtr. 6

Gtr. 3: w/ Rhy. Fig. 3 (7 times)
Gtr. 7: w/ Riff C (7 times)

E5   Aadd2   E5

spin-ning. Take me back to just be-fore I got diz-zy. Take me back,

11

GRAVEDIGGER

Words and Music by
David J. Matthews

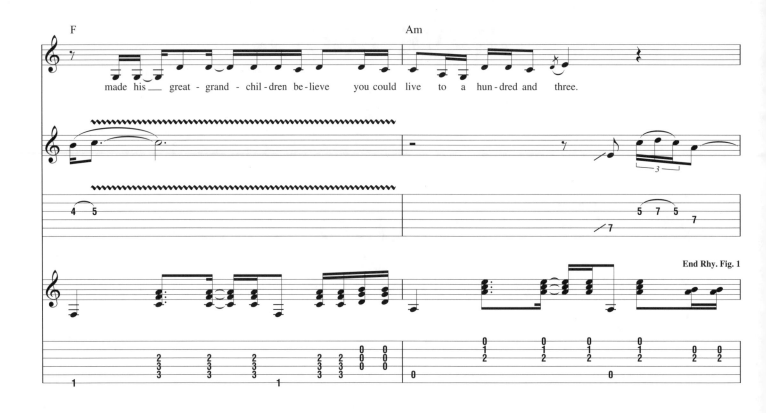

made his ___ great - grand - chil -dren be -lieve   you could live   to   a   hun -dred and   three.

End Rhy. Fig. 1

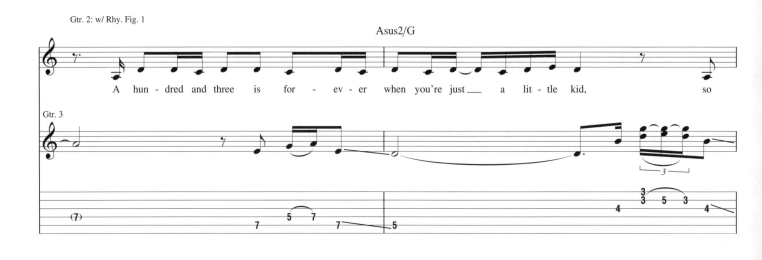

Gtr. 2: w/ Rhy. Fig. 1

Asus2/G

A   hun -dred and three   is   for - ev - er   when   you're just ___   a   lit - tle   kid,   so

Gtr. 3

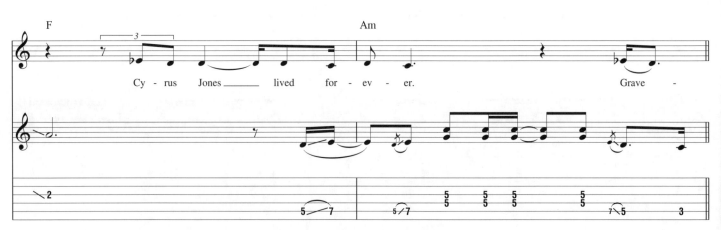

F   **Am**

Cy - rus   Jones ___   lived   for - ev - er.   Grave -

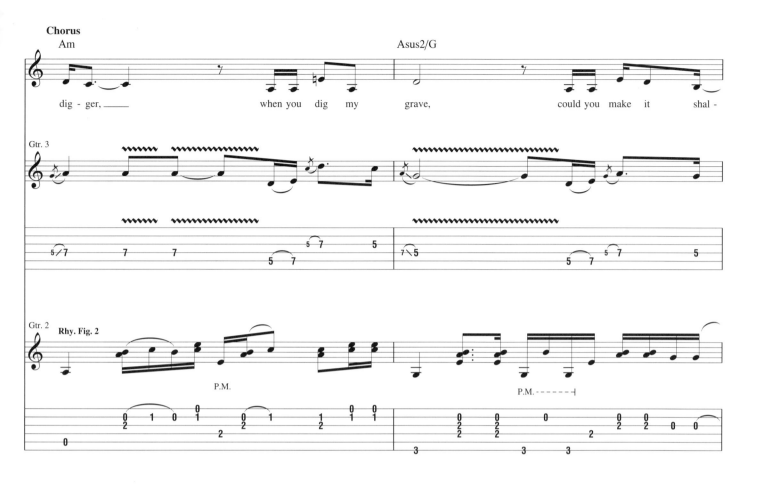

dig - ger, _____ when you dig my grave, could you make it shal -

- low _____ so that I _____ can feel _____ the rain? _____

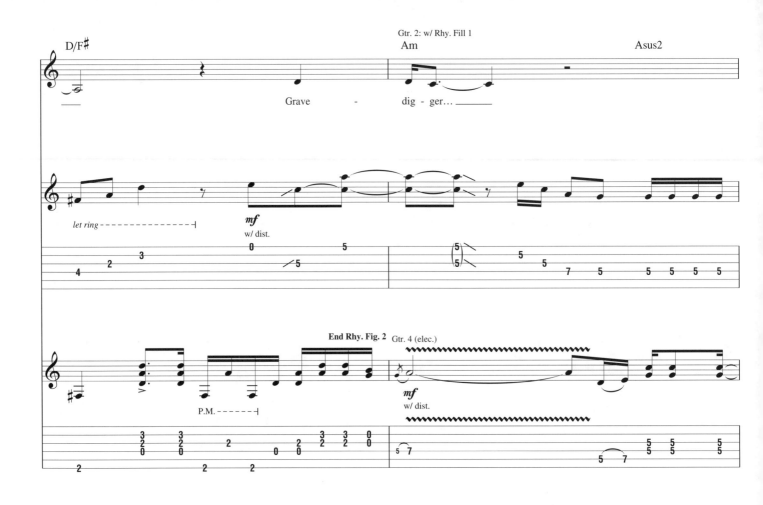

Verse

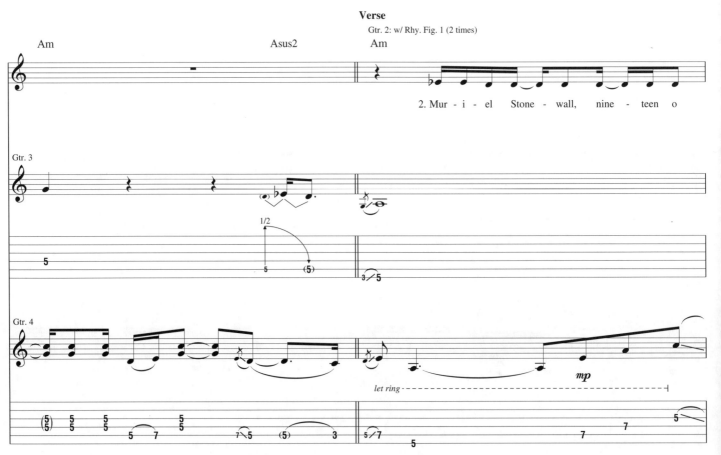

Chorus

Gtr. 2: w/ Rhy. Fig. 2

ba - bies. Grave - dig - ger, when you dig my

grave, could you make it shal - low so that I can feel the rain?

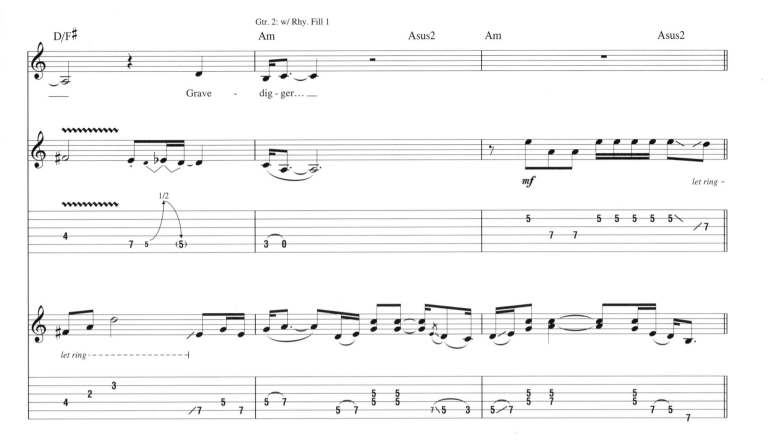

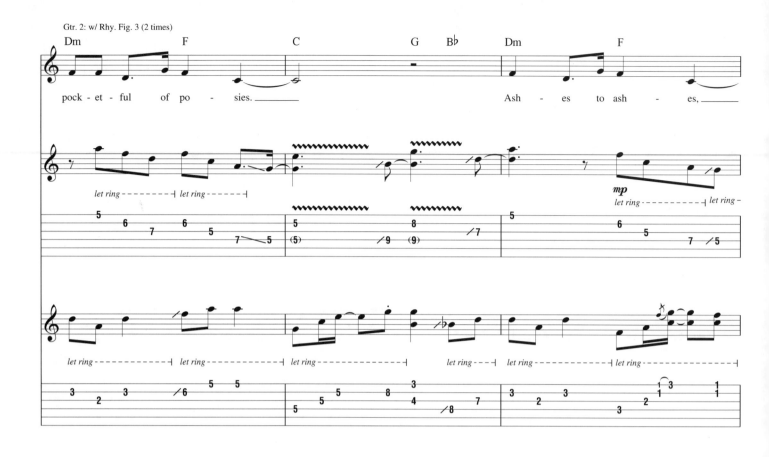

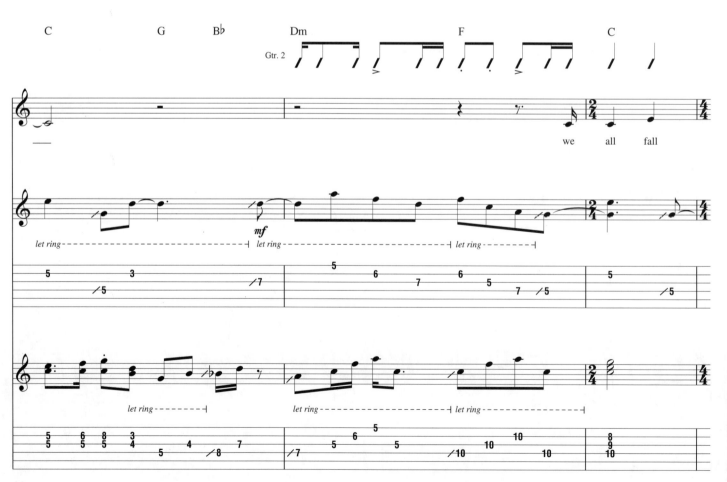

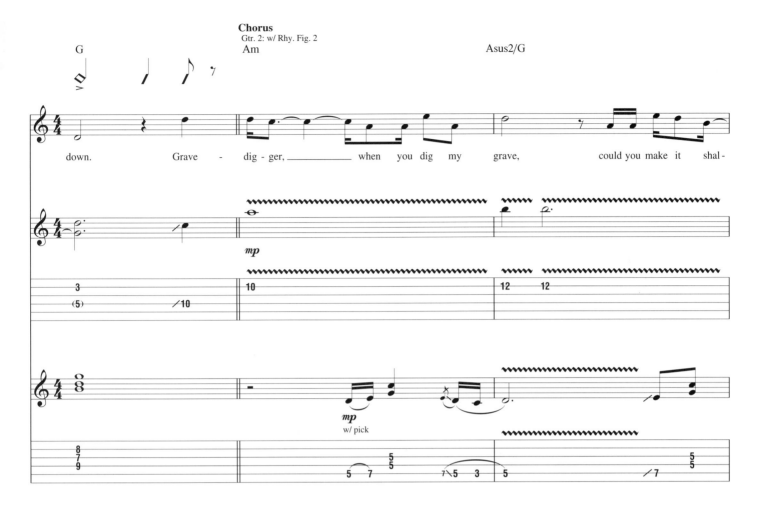

nine - ty - two. _____ Grave - dig - ger, _____ when you dig my

grave, _____ could you make it shal - low _____ so that I _____

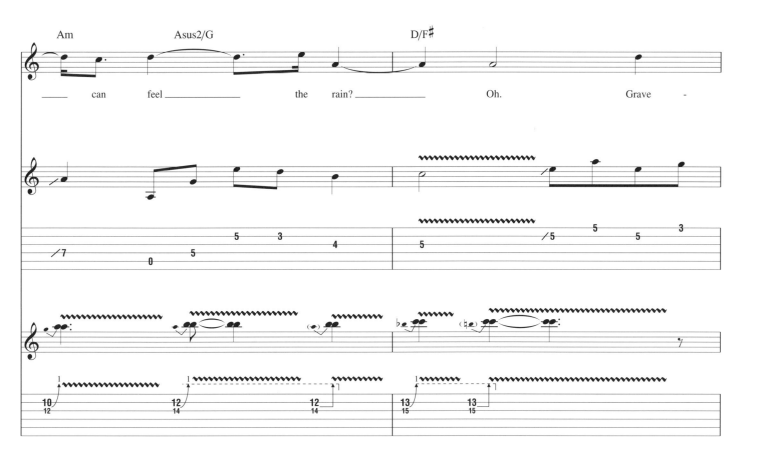

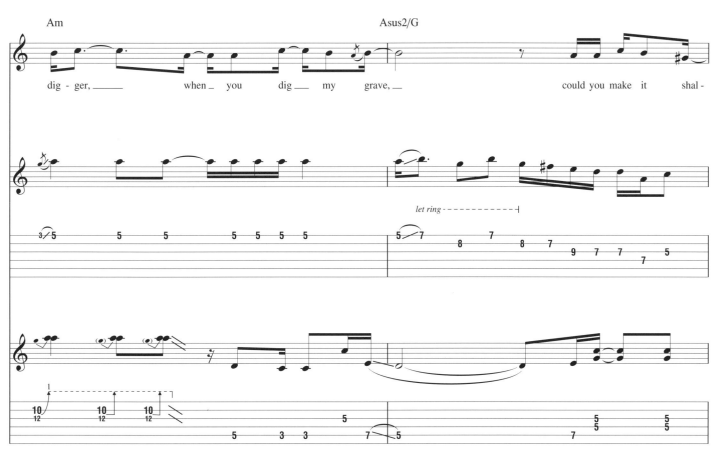

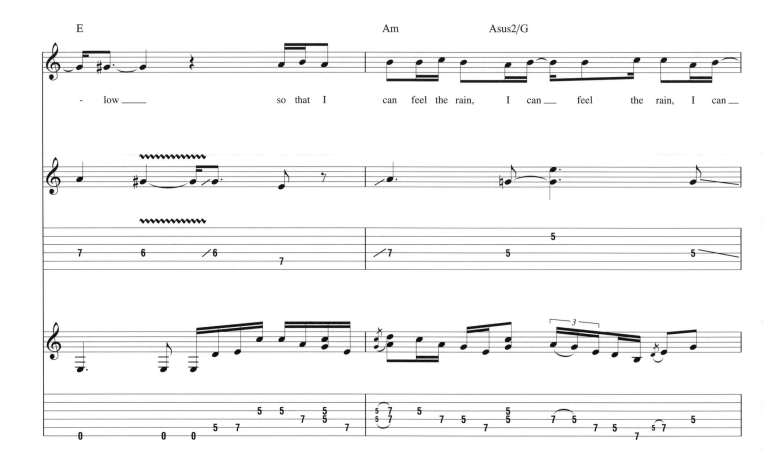

-low _____ so that I can feel the rain, I can _____ feel the rain, I can _____

Gtr. 2: w/ Rhy. Fig. 2 (1st 2 meas.)

_____ feel the rain? _____ Grave - dig - ger, _____ when _____ you dig my _____

Asus2/G

E

Gtr. 2

grave, _____ could you make it shal - low _____ so that I _____

Outro

*Gtr. 2: w/ Rhy. Fig. 2 (last 2 meas.)

Am   Asus2/G   D/F♯   Am   Asus2/G   F   E

Rhy. Fig. 4   End Rhy. Fig. 4

Gtr. 2

mp

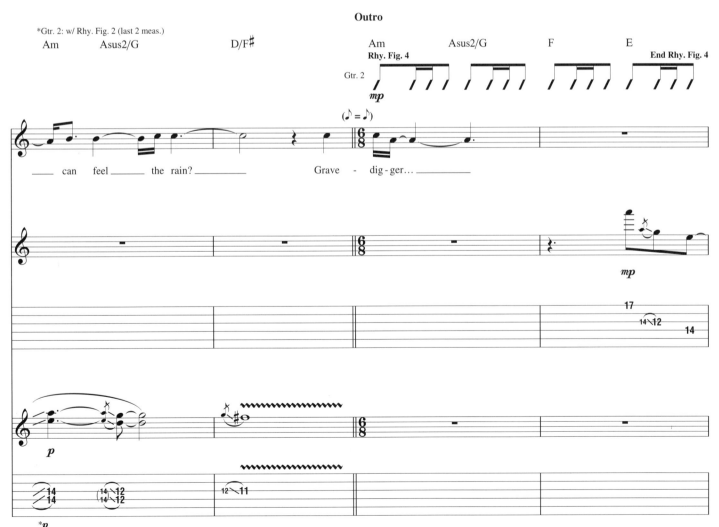

_____ can feel _____ the rain? _____ Grave - dig - ger... _____

Gtr. 2: w/ Rhy. Fig. 4 (2 1/2 times)

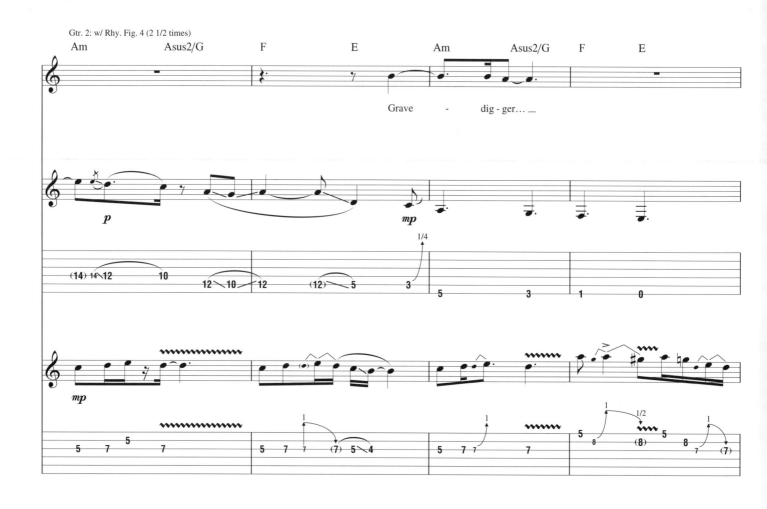

Grave - dig - ger... __

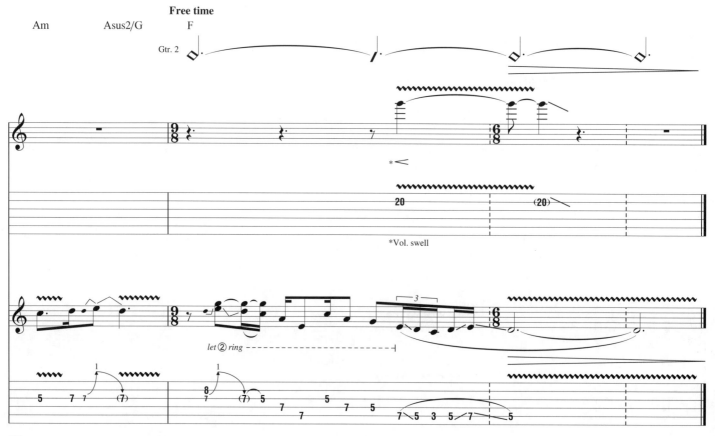

SOME DEVIL

Words and Music by
David J. Matthews

TROUBLE

Words by David J. Matthews
Music by David J. Matthews
and Stephen Harris

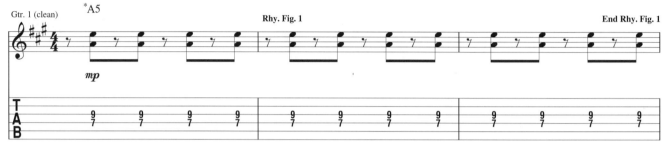

*Chord symbols reflect overall harmony.

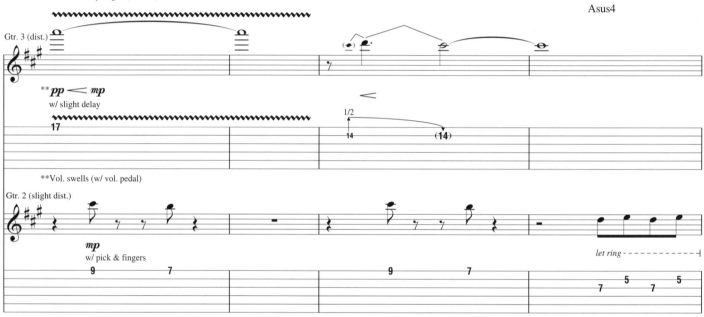

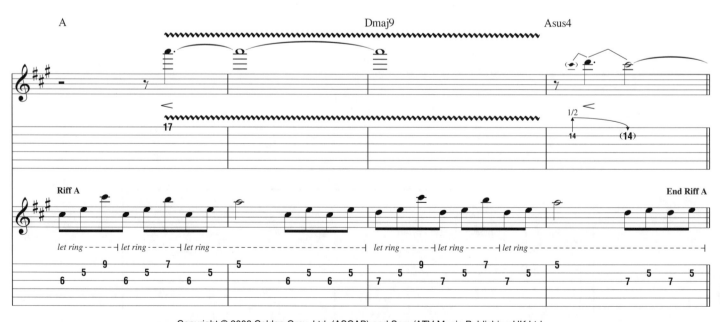

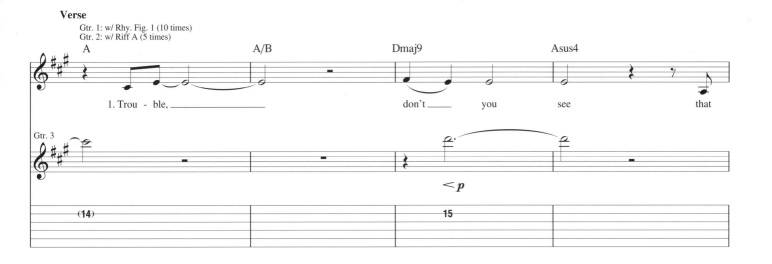

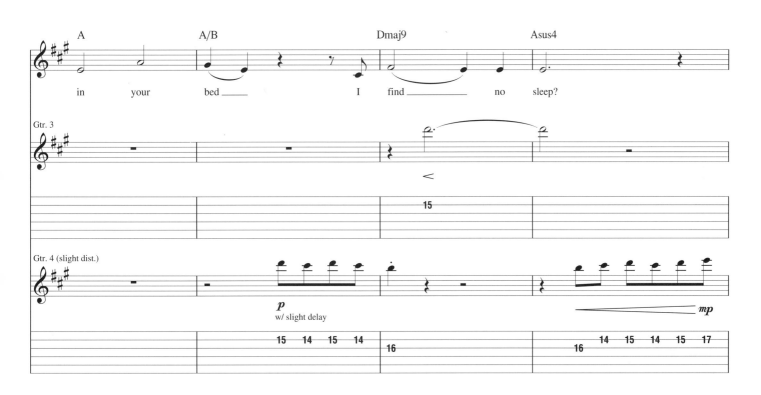

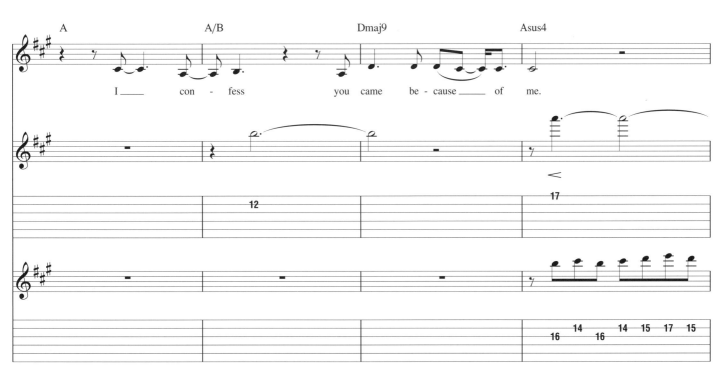

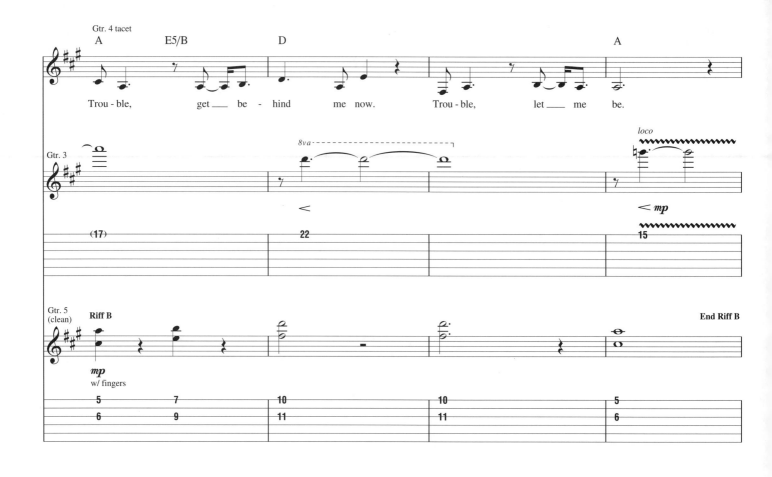

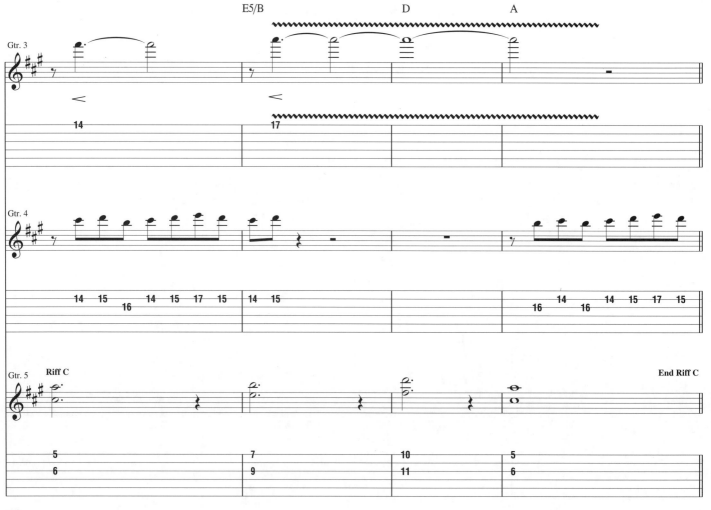

You know ___ too ___ well ___ it was me that ⌈ called ___ you ___ here. ___ ⌉
⌊ brought ___ you ___ here. ___ Oh. ⌋

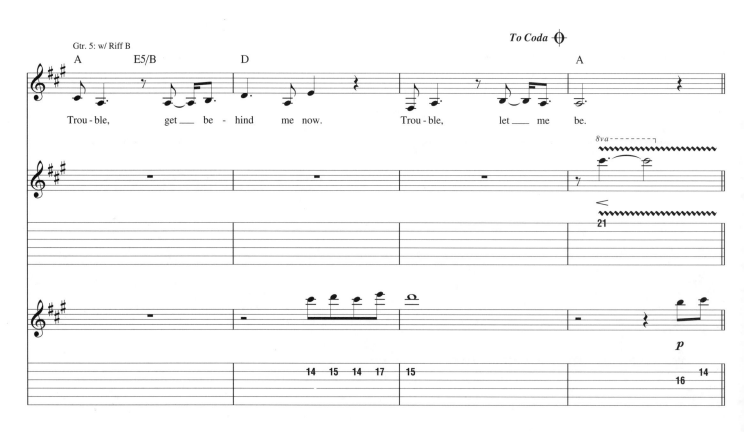

Trou - ble, get ___ be - hind me now. Trou - ble, let ___ me be.

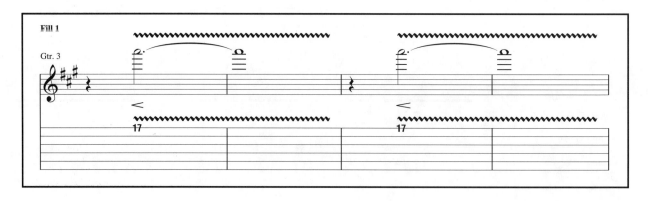

Bridge

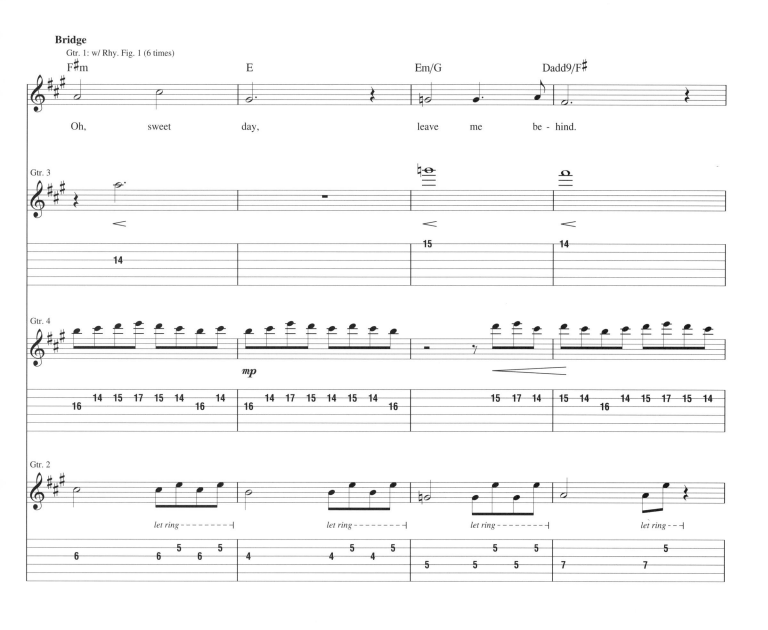

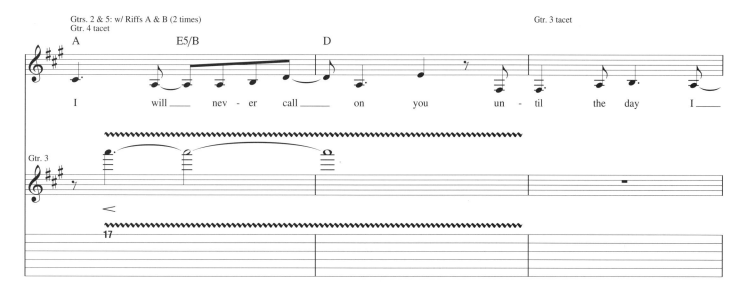

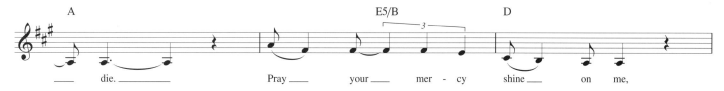

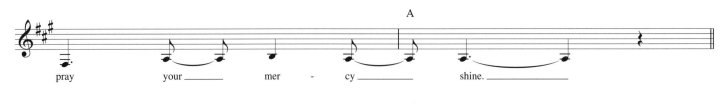

pray   your ____ mer - cy ____ shine. ____

Bridge

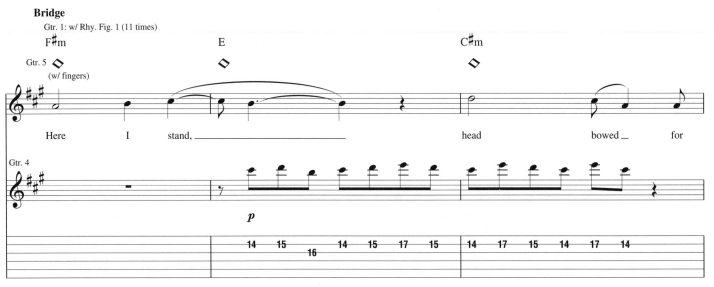

Gtr. 1: w/ Rhy. Fig. 1 (11 times)

Here   I   stand, ____ head   bowed ___ for

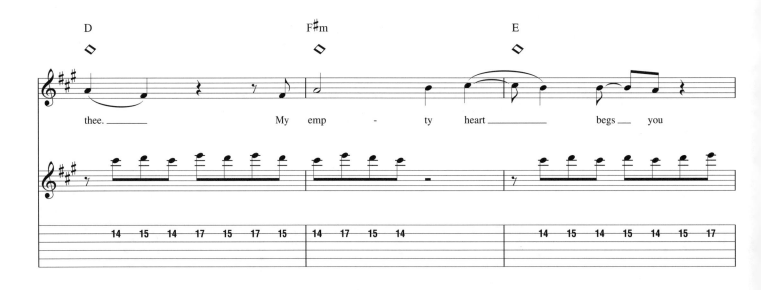

thee. ____ My emp - ty heart ____ begs ___ you

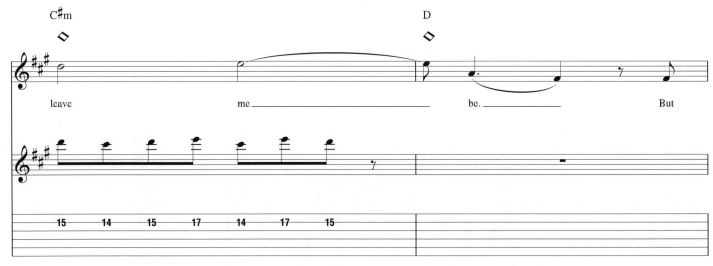

leave   me ____ be. ____ But

Trou - ble,   I'll __ not   trou - ble thee. _   Let __   your _ mer - cy shine. _____

Interlude

Gtr. 1: w/ Rhy. Fig. 1 (4 times)

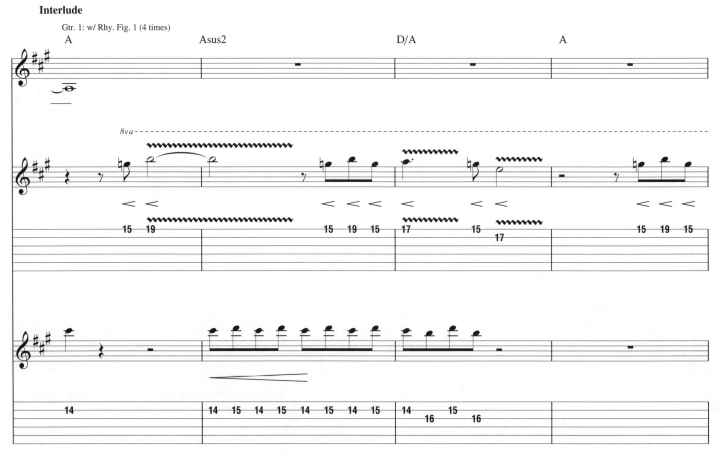

40

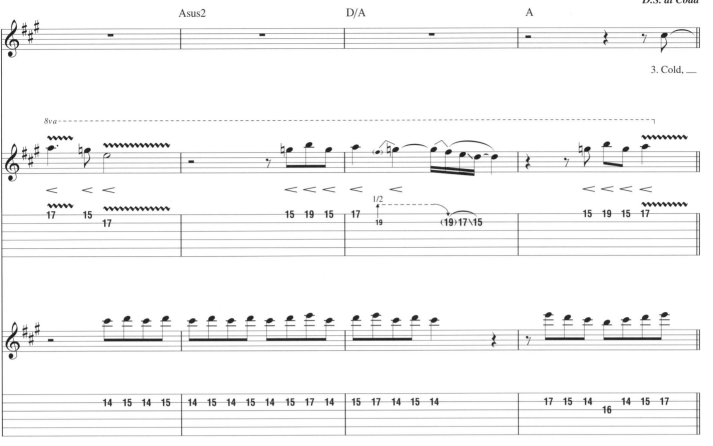

3. Cold, __

✛ Coda

Gtr. 1: w/ Rhy. Fig. 1 (till end)
Gtr. 2: w/ Riff A (1st 3 meas.)
Gtr. 5: w/ Riff C (3 times)

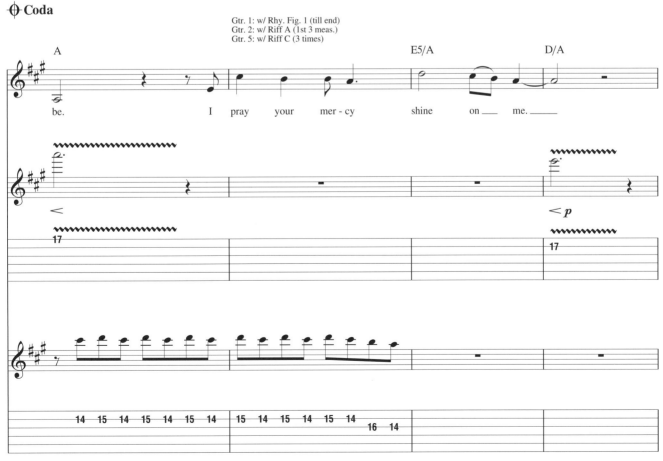

be.   I pray your mer - cy shine on __ me. __

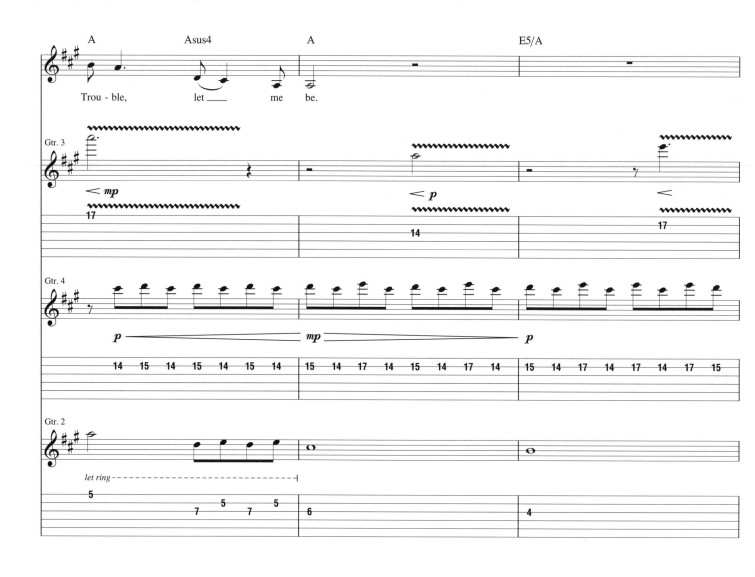

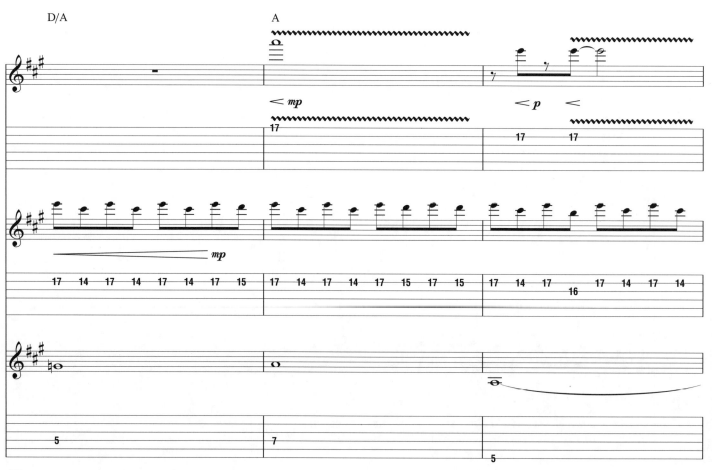

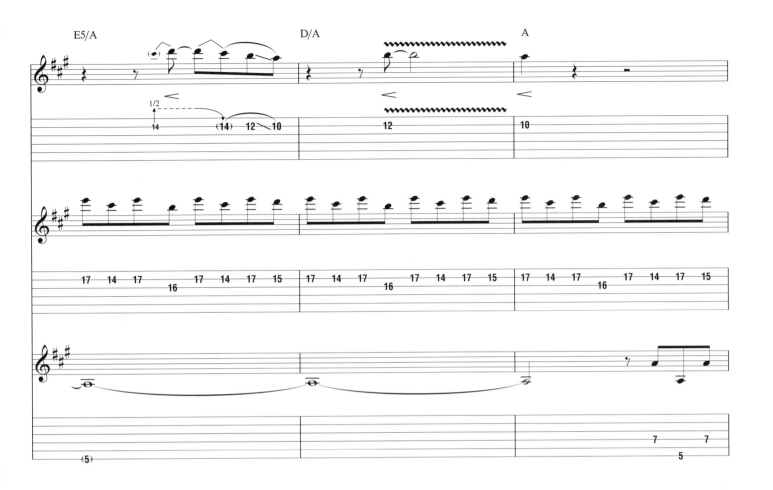

Gtr. 5: w/ Riff B

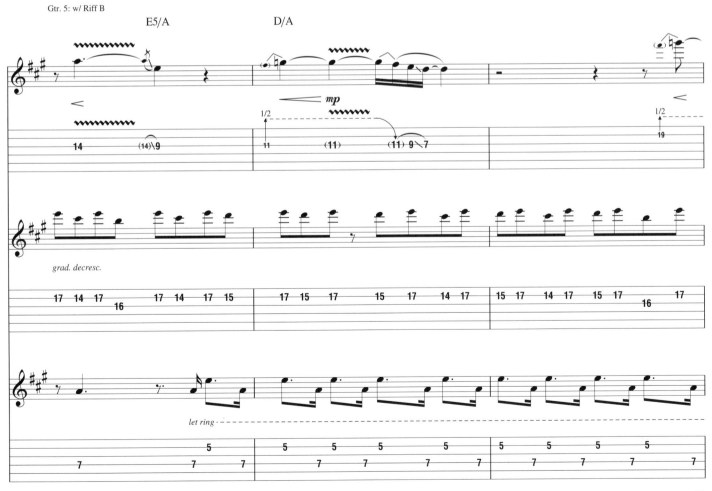

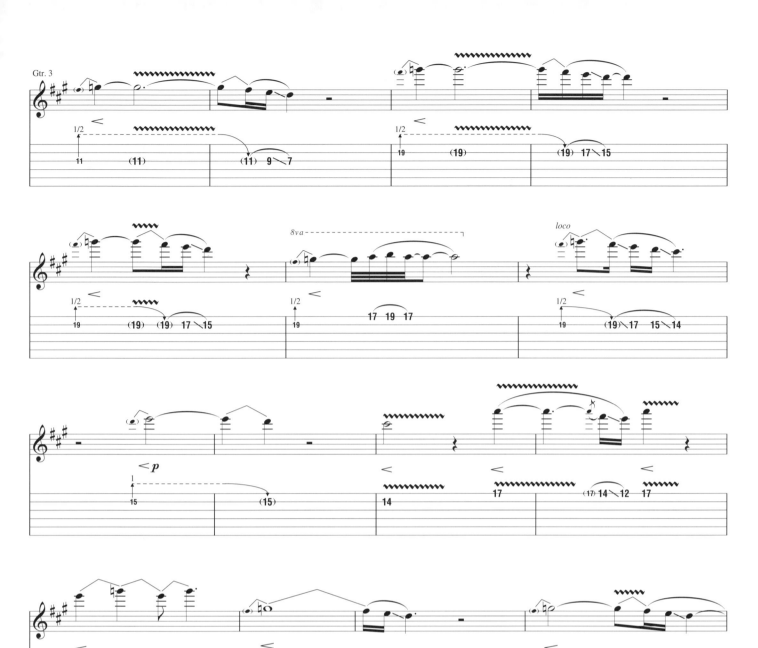

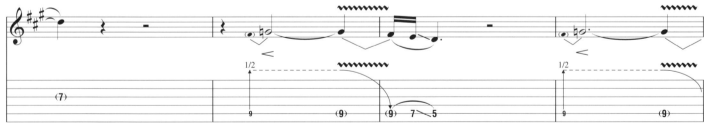

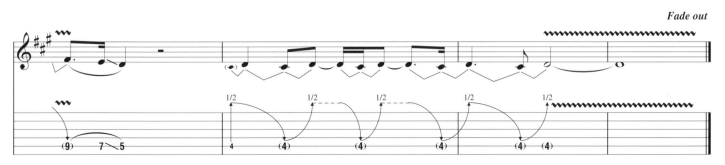

GREY BLUE EYES

Words by David J. Matthews
Music by David J. Matthews,
Trey Anastasio and Stephen Harris

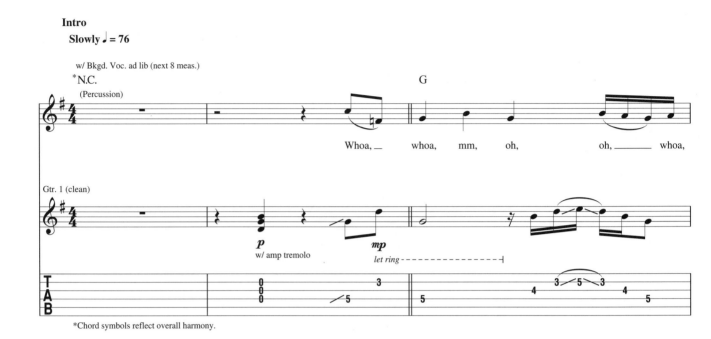

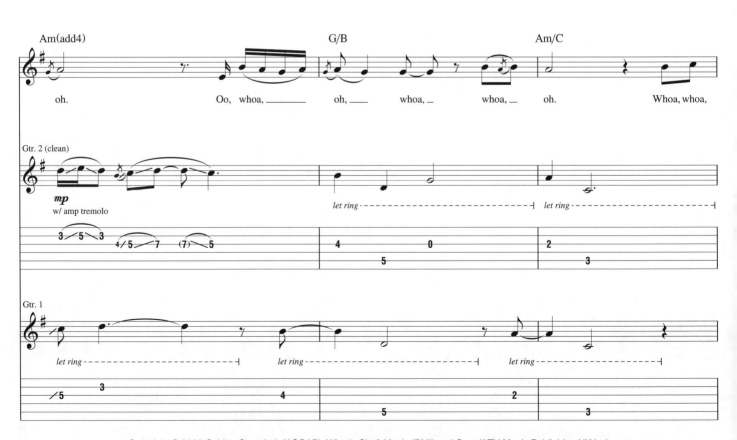

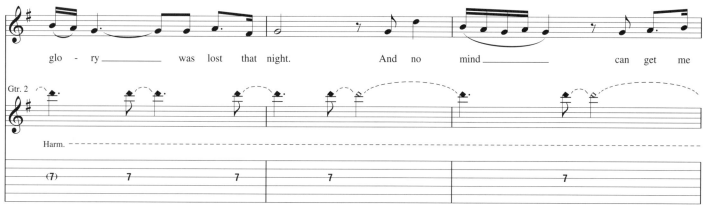

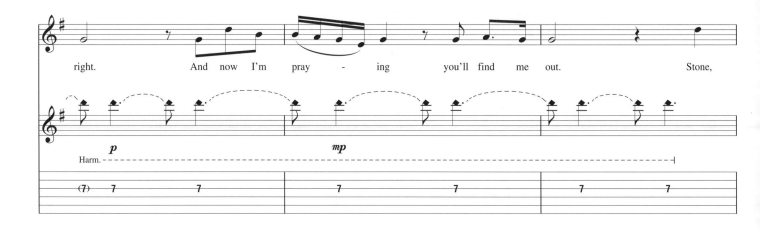

right. And now I'm pray - ing you'll find me out. Stone,

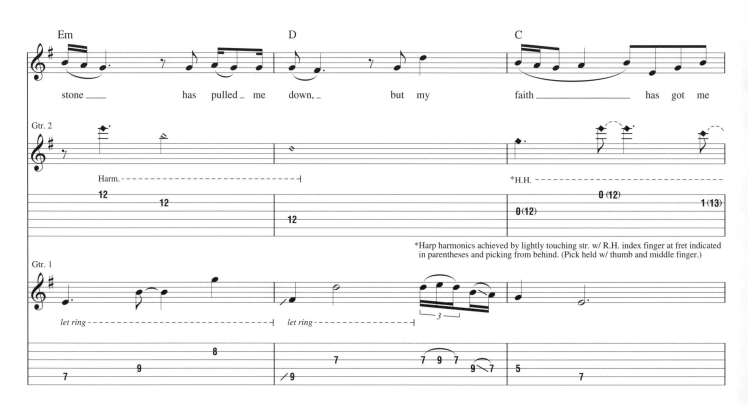

stone _____ has pulled _ me down, _ but my faith _____ has got me

*Harp harmonics achieved by lightly touching str. w/ R.H. index finger at fret indicated in parentheses and picking from behind. (Pick held w/ thumb and middle finger.)

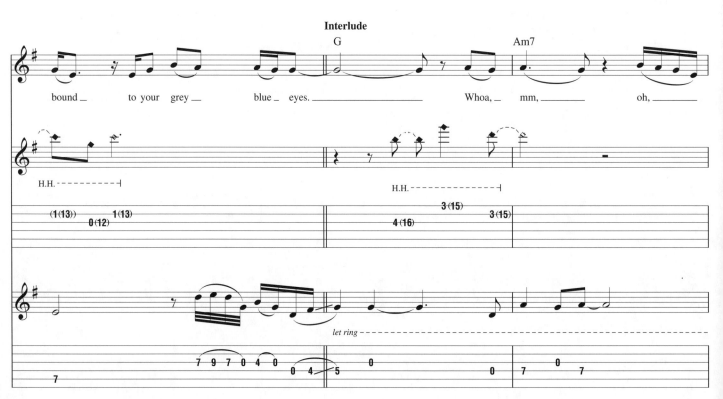

Interlude

bound _ to your grey _ blue _ eyes. _____ Whoa, _ mm, _____ oh, _____

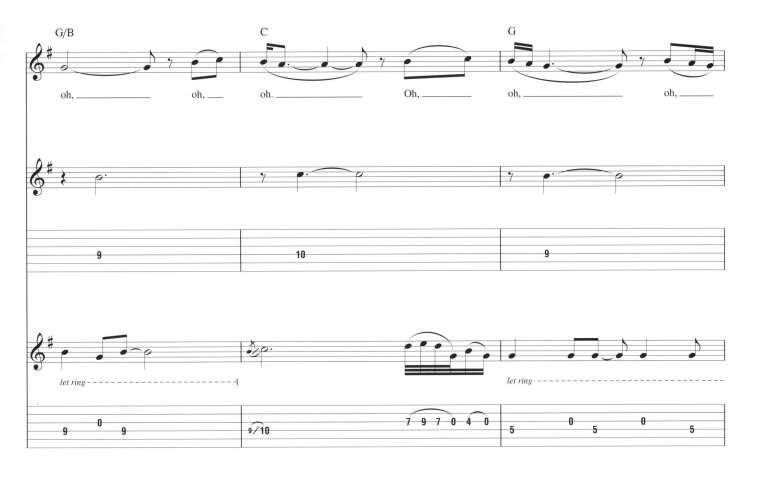

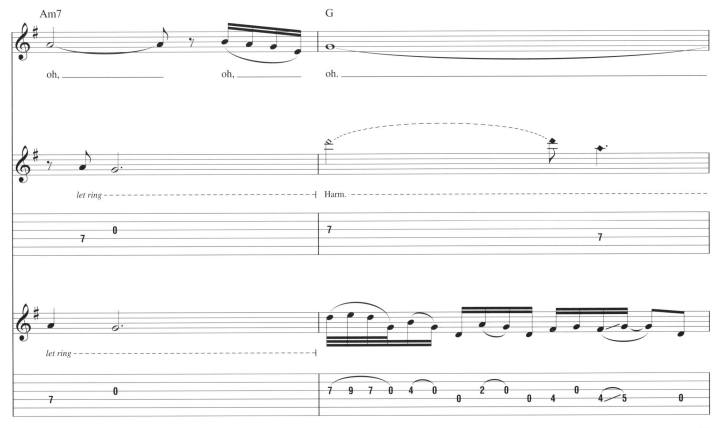

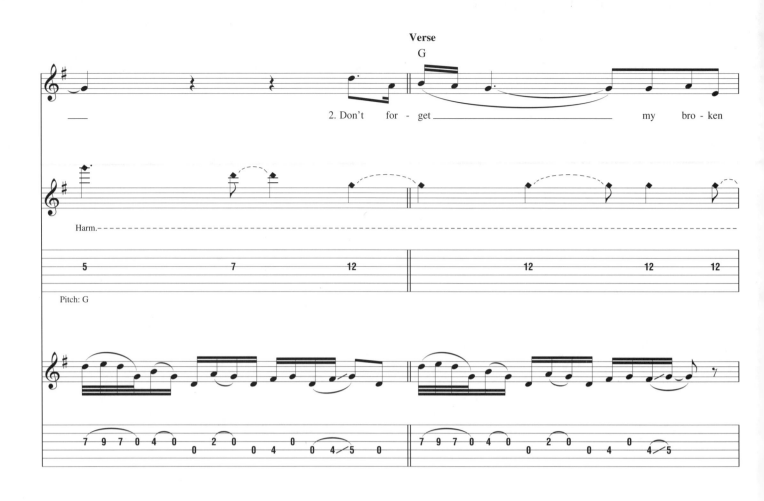

2. Don't for - get _____ my bro - ken

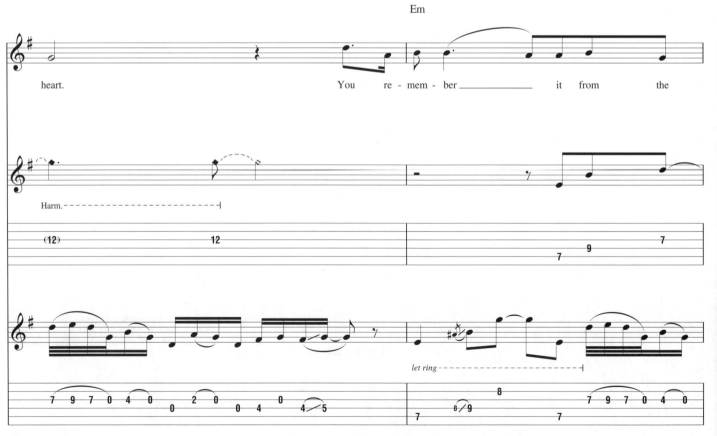

heart.   You re - mem - ber _____ it from the

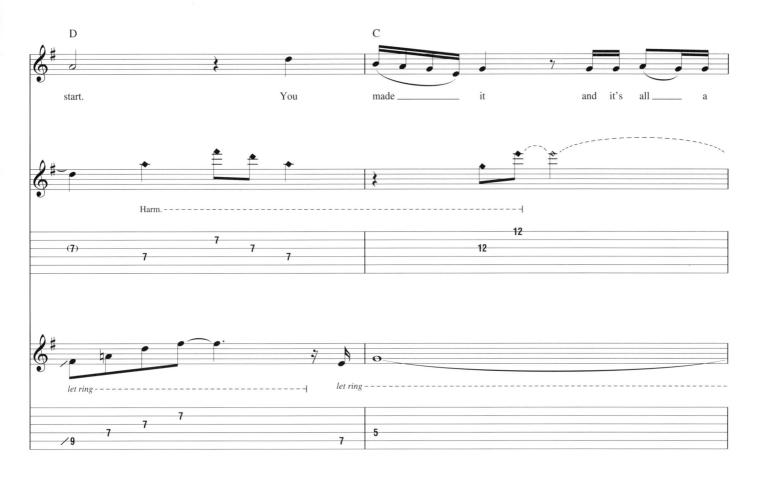

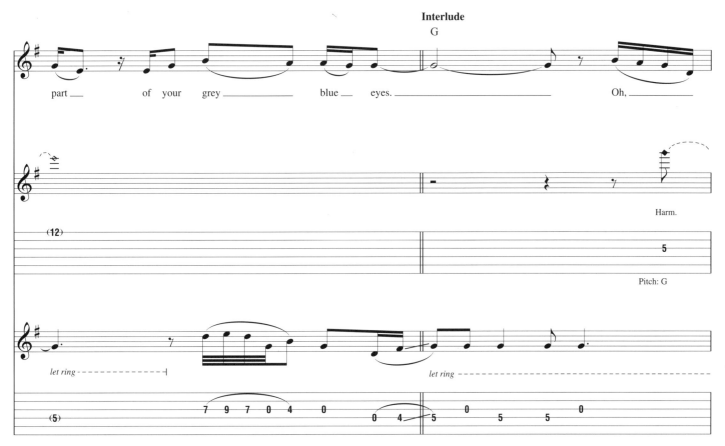

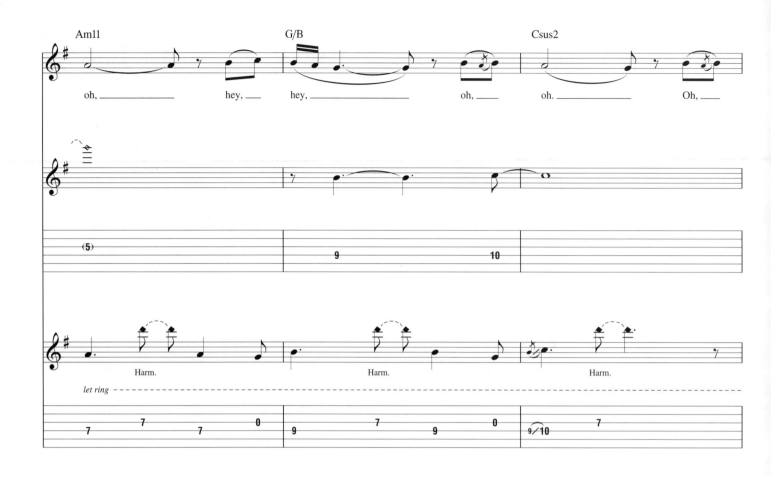

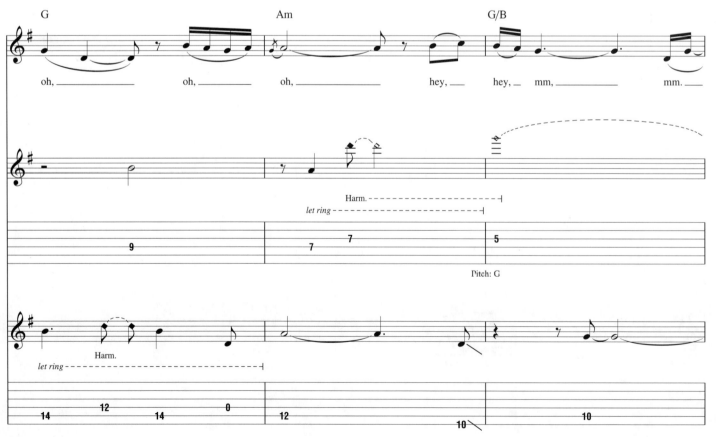

Outro-Verse

w/ Bkgd. Voc. ad lib (next 4 meas.)

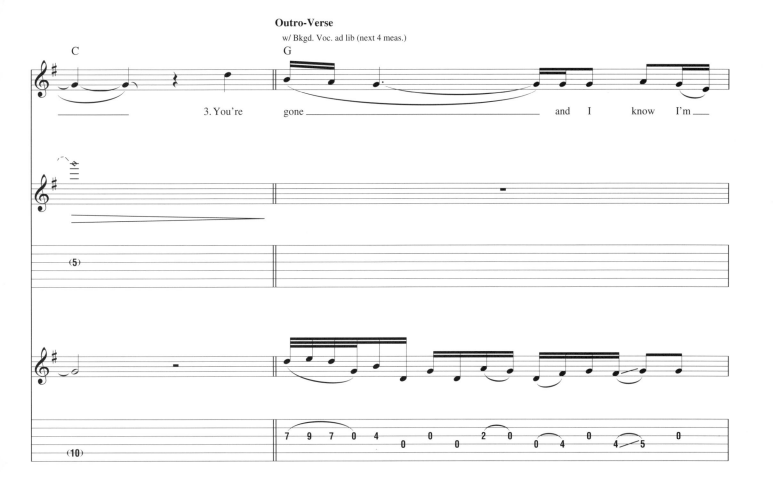

3. You're gone _____ and I know I'm ___

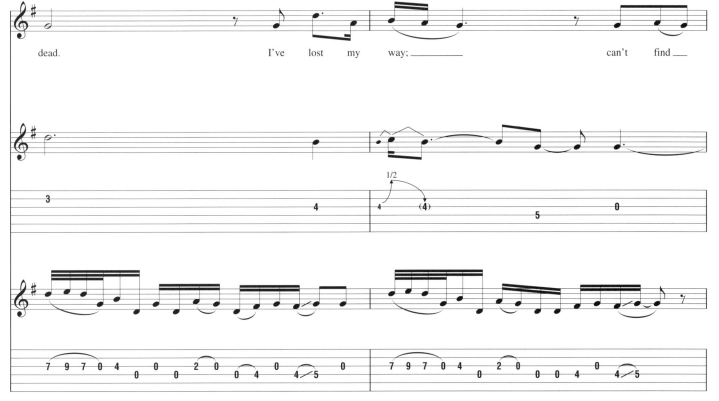

dead.   I've lost my way; _____   can't find ___

it　　　　　in　your　grey _____ blue _ eyes, _____　　　　　grey _ blue _

Harm. - - - - - - - - - - - -

Pitch: G

let ring - - - - - - - - - - - - - - - -

Harm.

let ring - - - - - - - - - - - -

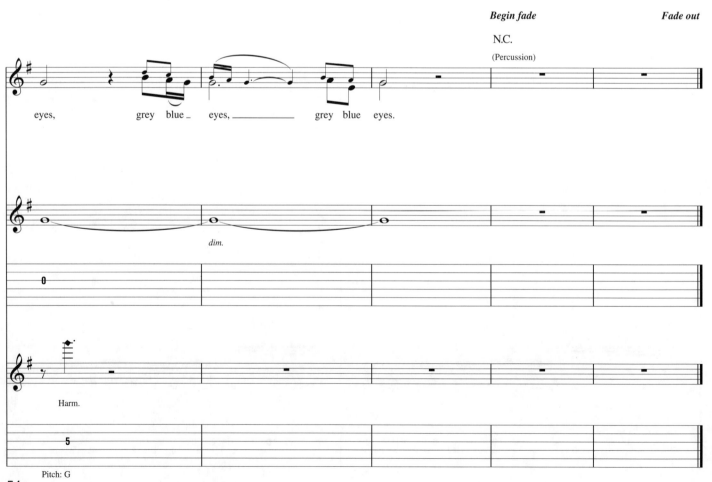

Begin fade　　　**Fade out**

N.C.

(Percussion)

eyes,　　　　grey blue _ eyes, _____　　　grey blue eyes.

dim.

Harm.

Pitch: G

SAVE ME

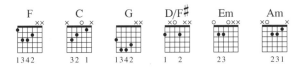

Words and Music by
David J. Matthews

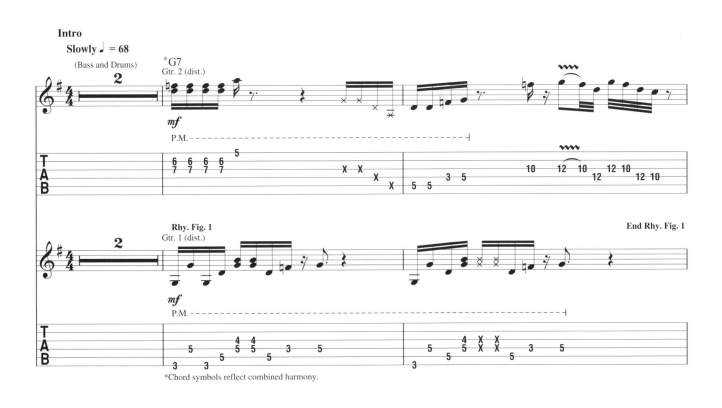

*Chord symbols reflect combined harmony.

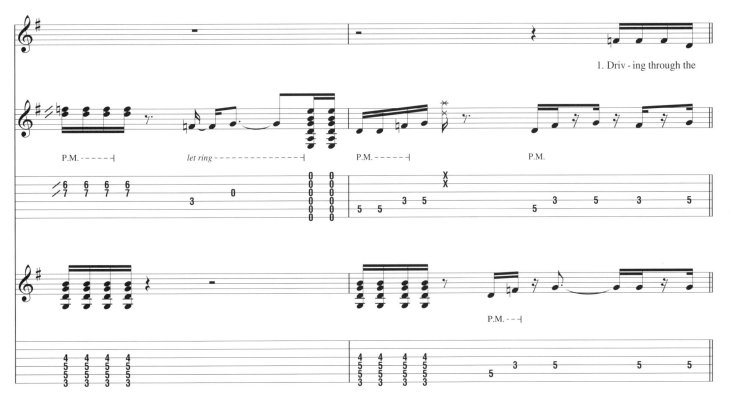

1. Driv-ing through the

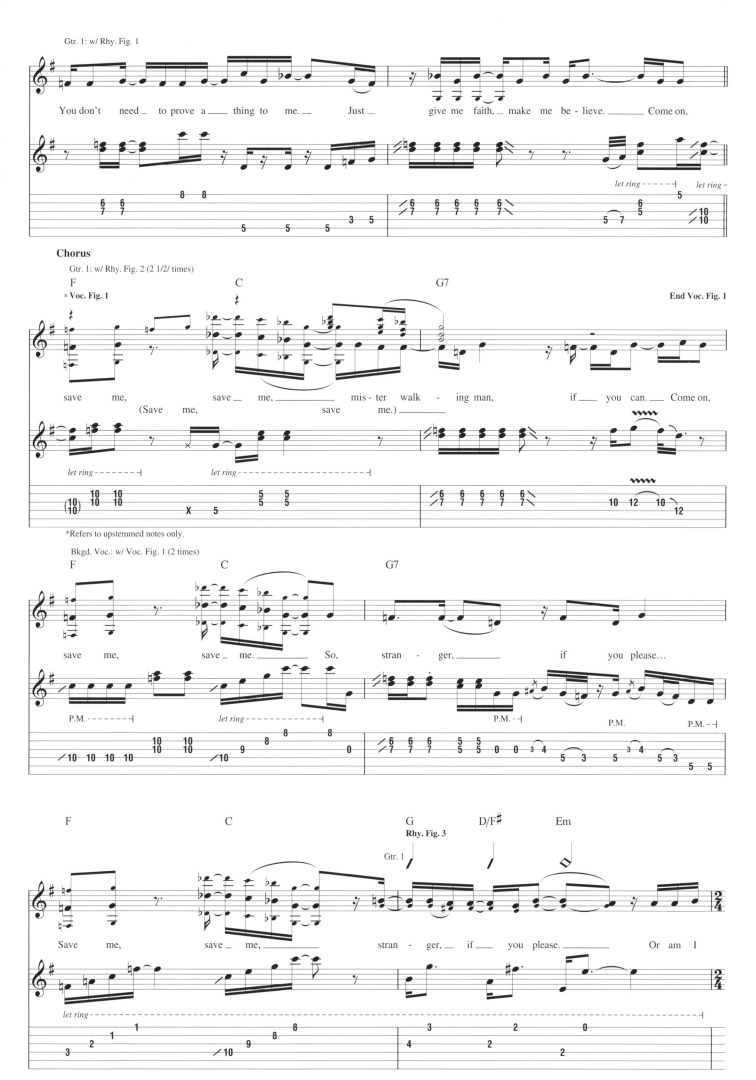

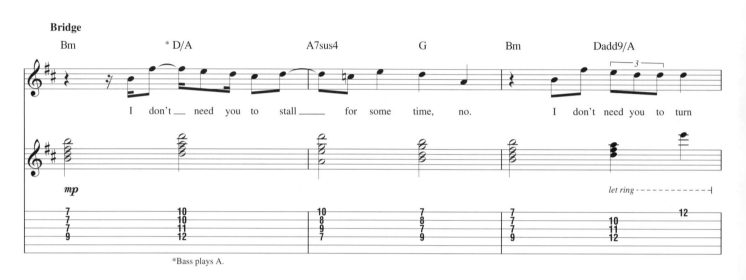

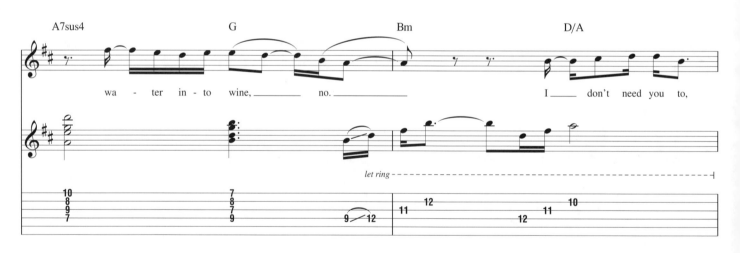

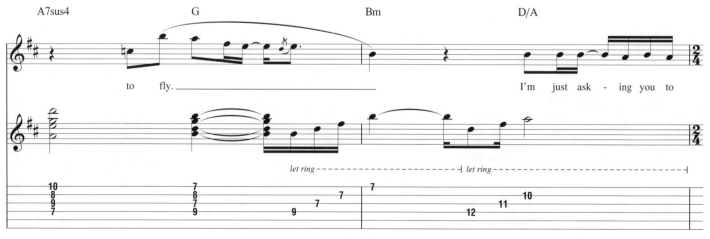

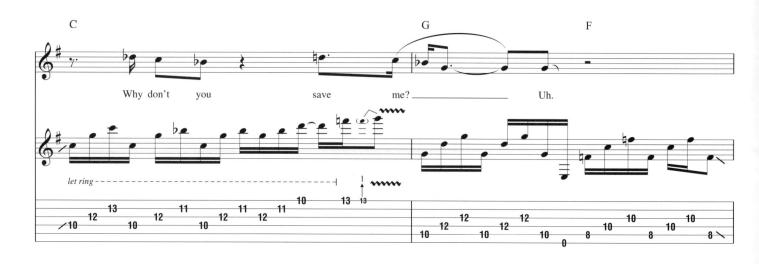

Why don't you save me? _____ Uh.

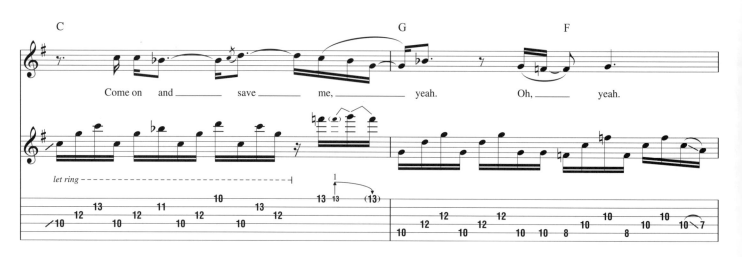

Come on and _____ save _____ me, _____ yeah. Oh, _____ yeah.

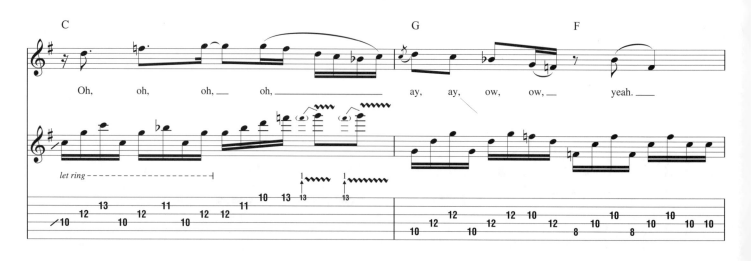

Oh, oh, oh, __ oh, _____ ay, ay, ow, ow, __ yeah. ____

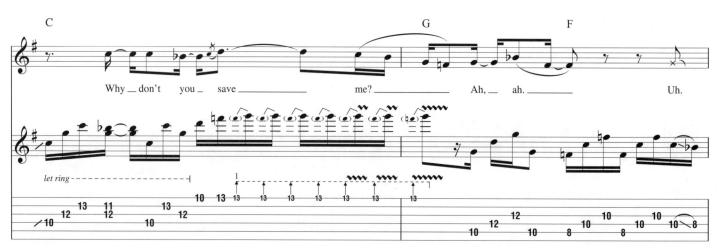

Why __ don't you __ save _____ me? _____ Ah, __ ah. _____ Uh.

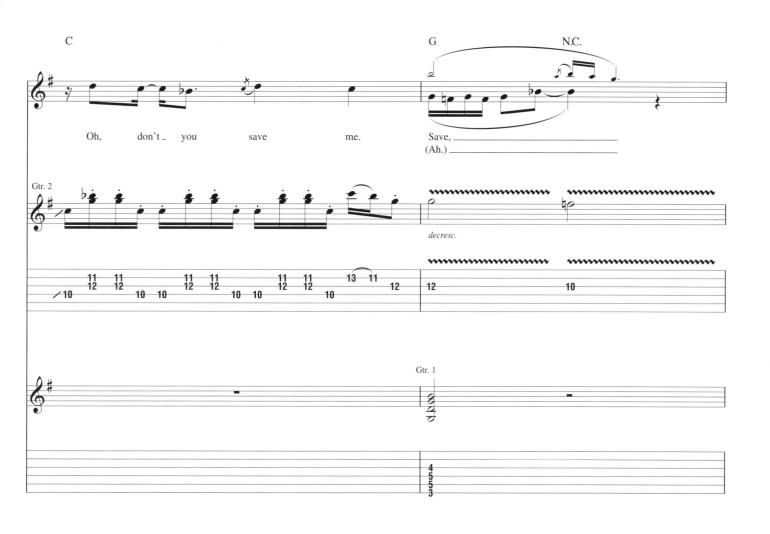

Oh, don't you save me. Save, _____
(Ah.) _____

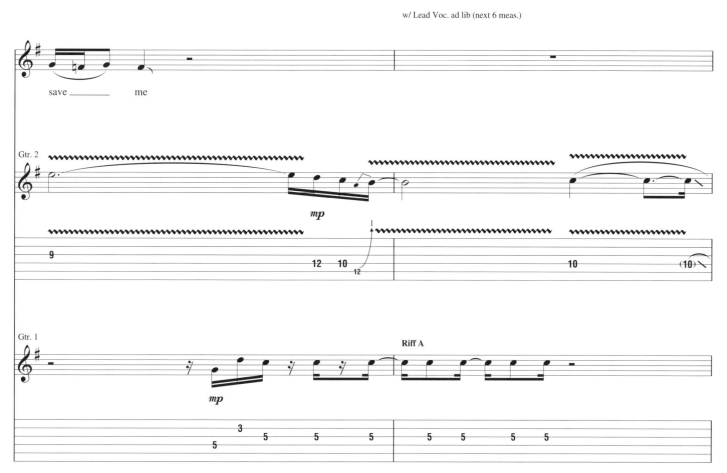

save _____ me

Ah,   ah,   ah. _____   Ah,   ah,   ah. _____

Ah,   ah,   ah. _____   Ah,   ah,   ah.) _____

STAY OR LEAVE

Words and Music by
David J. Matthews

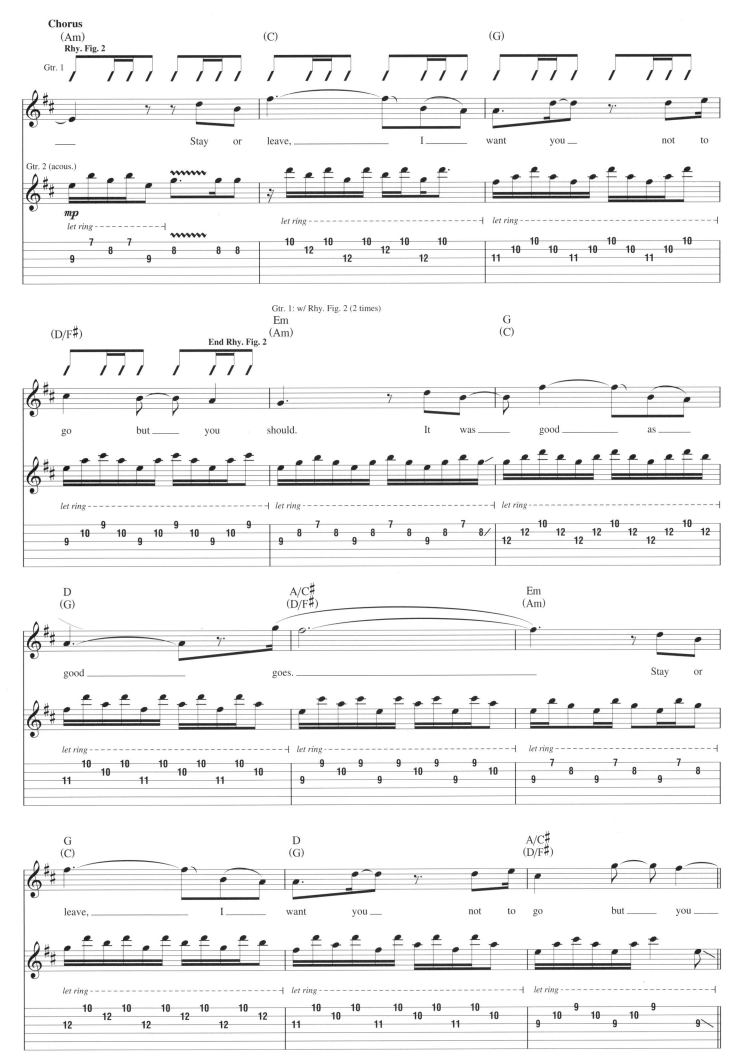

Interlude
w/ Bkgd. Voc. ad lib (next 8 meas.)
Gtr. 1: w/ Rhy. Fig 1

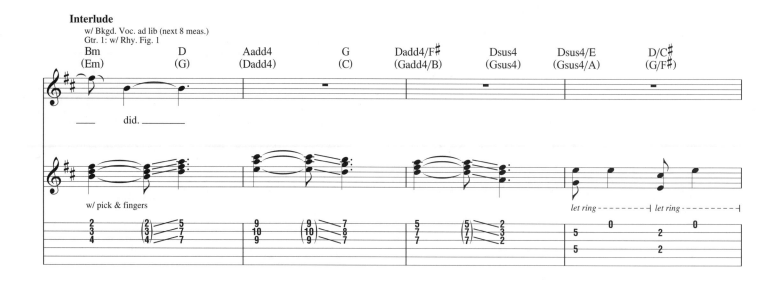

did.

w/ pick & fingers

let ring let ring

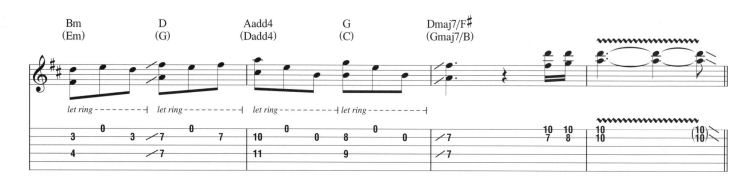

let ring let ring let ring let ring

Verse
Gtr. 1: w/ Rhy. Fig. 1 (2 times)
Gtr. 2 tacet

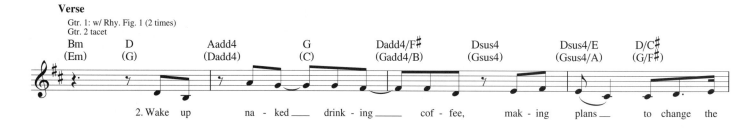

2. Wake up na - ked drink - ing cof - fee, mak - ing plans to change the

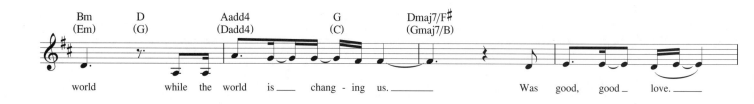

world while the world is chang - ing us. Was good, good love.

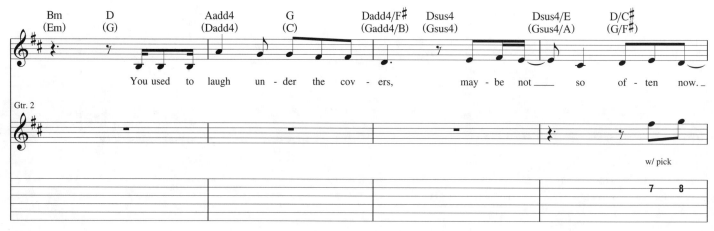

You used to laugh un - der the cov - ers, may - be not so of - ten now.

Gtr. 2

w/ pick

Chorus

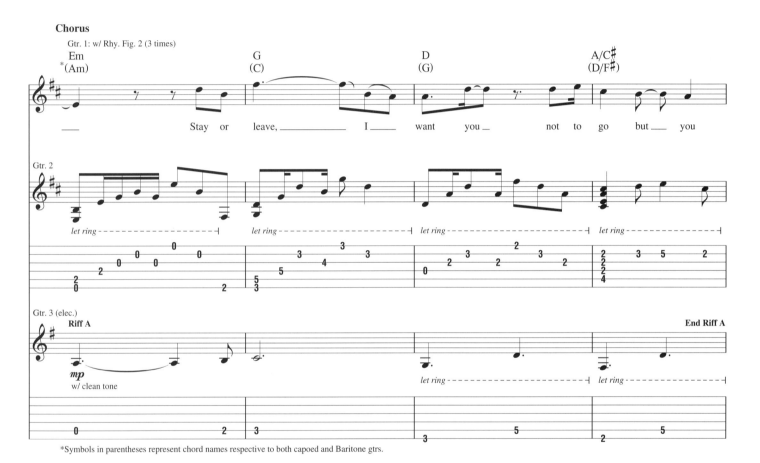

*Symbols in parentheses represent chord names respective to both capoed and Baritone gtrs.

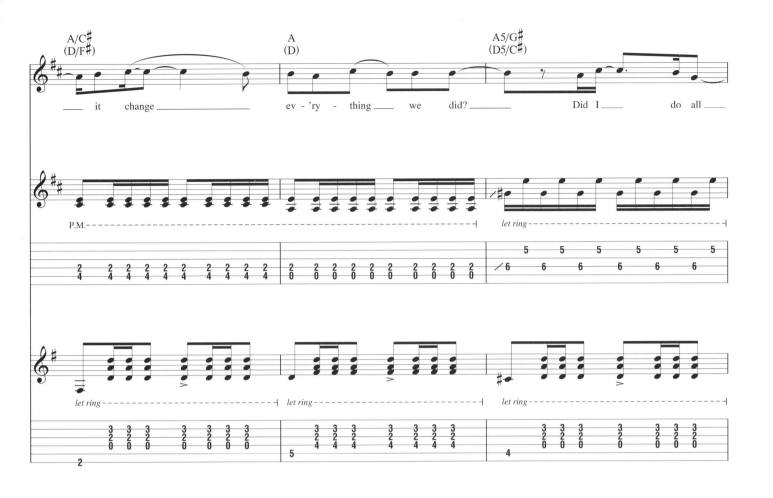

Interlude

Gtr. 1: w/ Rhy. Fig. 1 (1st 5 meas.)

AN' ANOTHER THING

Words and Music by
David J. Matthews

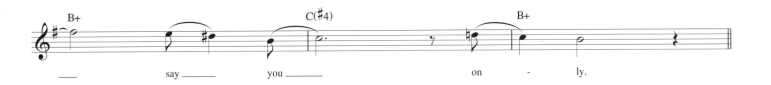

Chorus

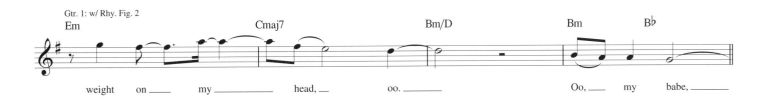

Interlude

Verse

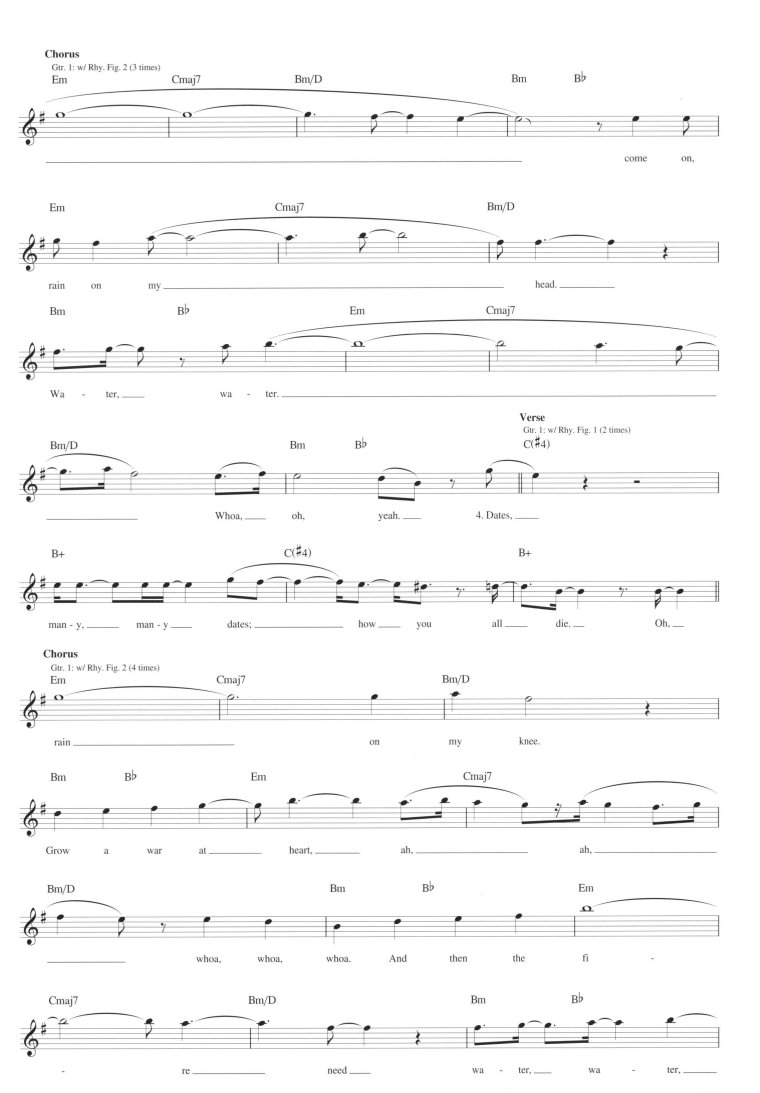

OH

Words and Music by
David J. Matthews

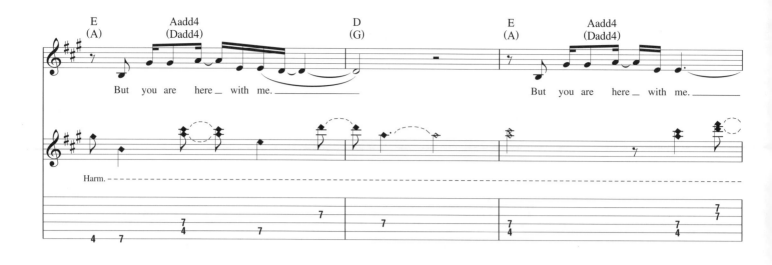

But you are here __ with me. _____   But you are here __ with me. _____

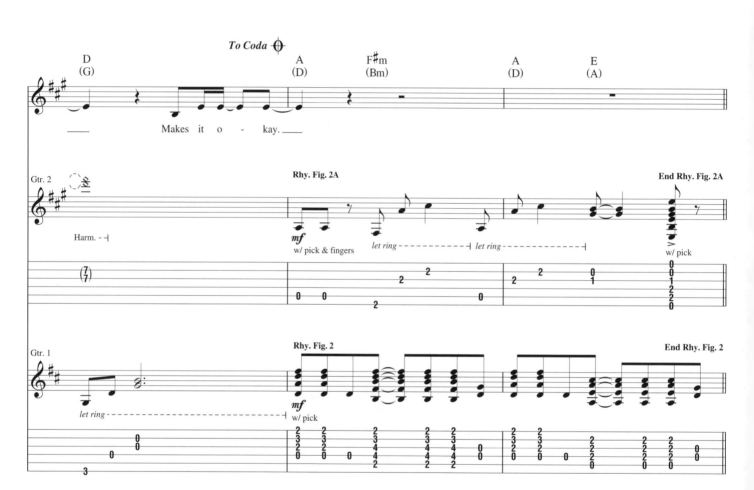

Makes it o - kay. ___

Pre-Chorus

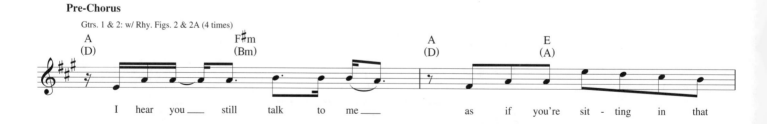

I hear you __ still talk to me ___   as if you're sit - ting in that

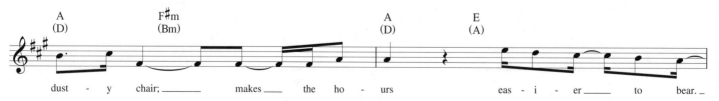

dust - y chair; ___   makes ___ the ho - urs   eas - i - er ___ to bear.

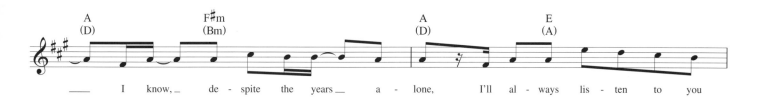

I know,__ de-spite the years__ a-lone, I'll al-ways lis-ten to you

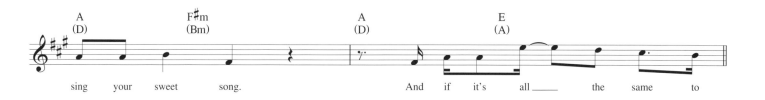

sing your sweet song. And if it's all __ the same to

Chorus

you, I love __ you, oh, __ so well, like a kid loves can-dy and __ fresh

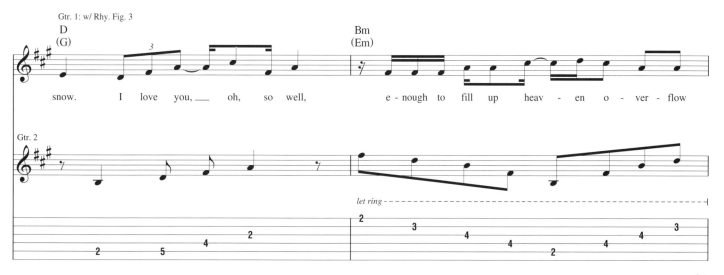

snow. I love you, __ oh, so well, e-nough to fill up heav-en o-ver-flow

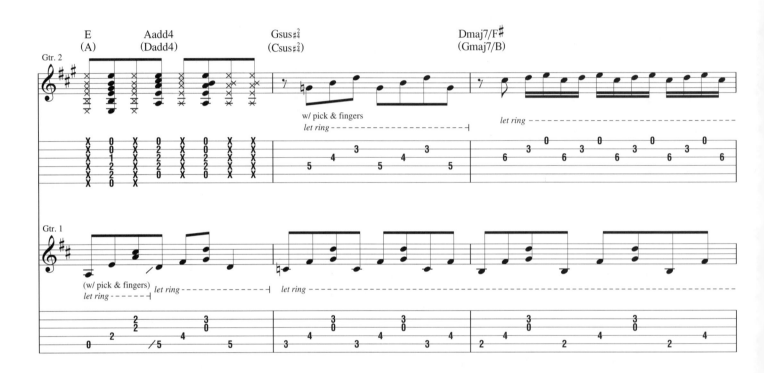

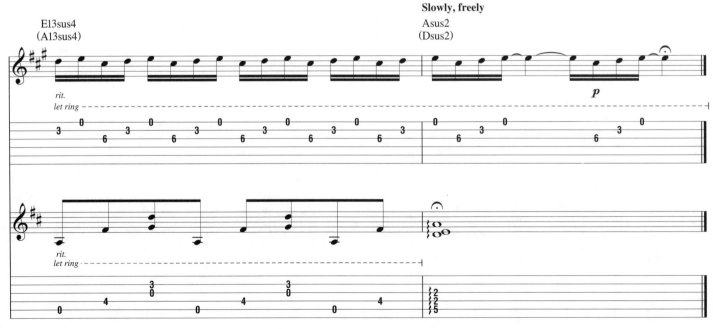

BABY

Words and Music by
David J. Matthews

*Chord symbols reflect basic harmony.

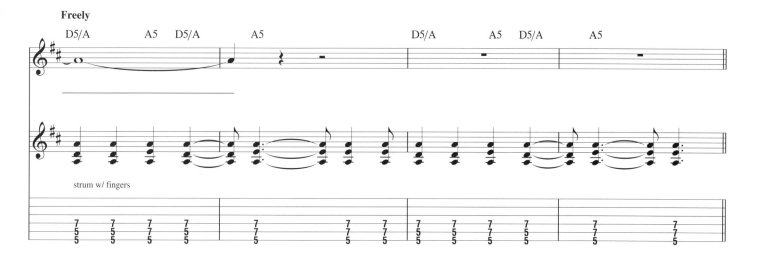

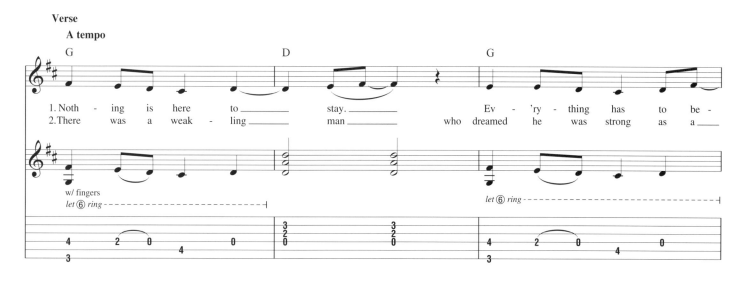

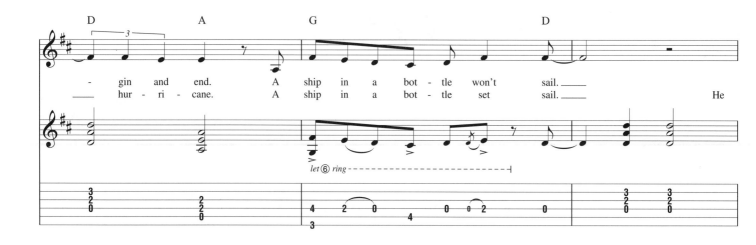

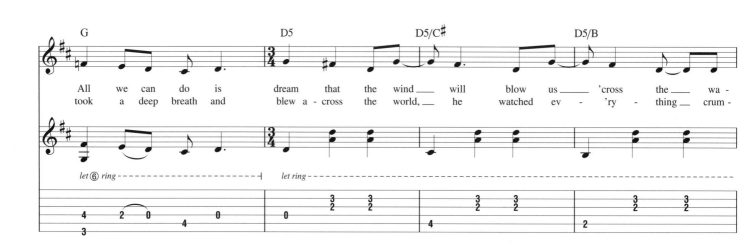

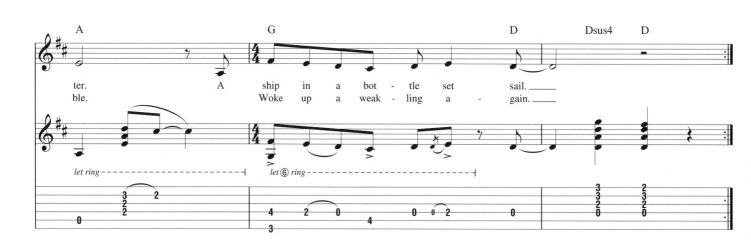

Bridge

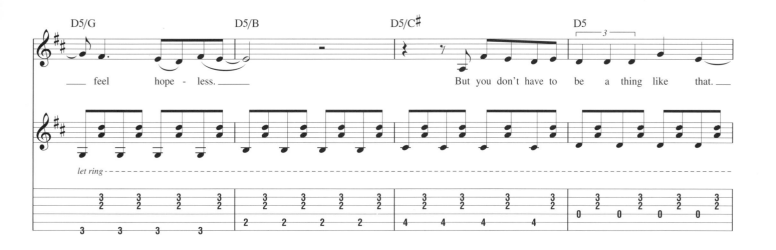

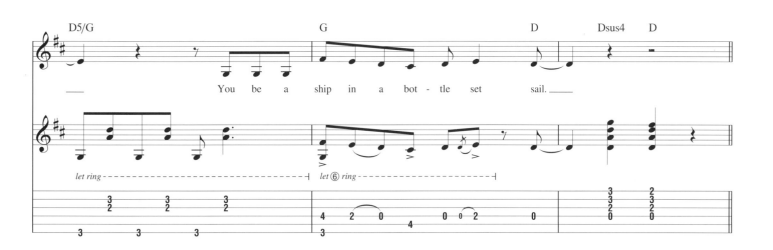

Chorus

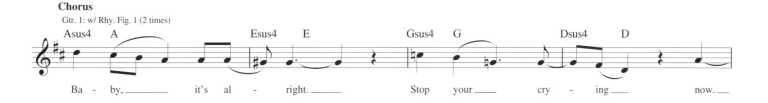

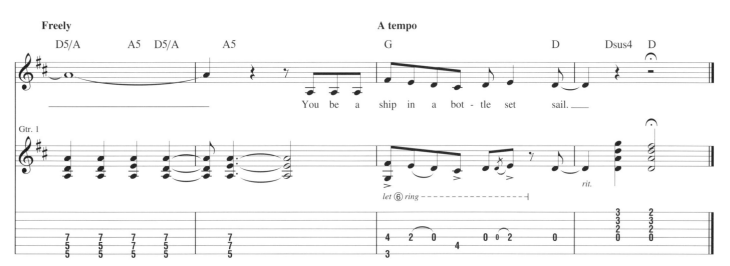

UP AND AWAY

Words and Music by
David J. Matthews

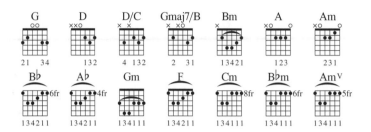

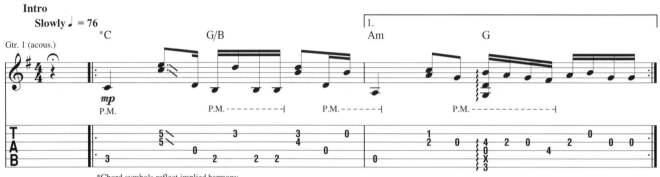

*Chord symbols reflect implied harmony.

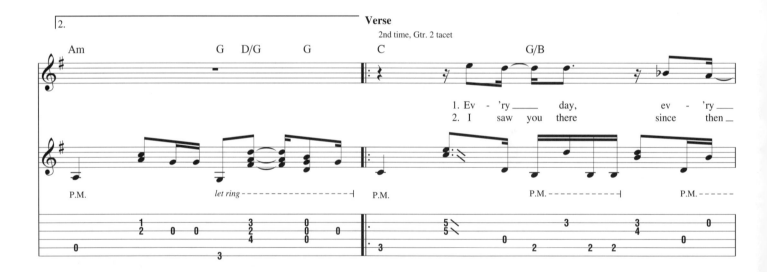

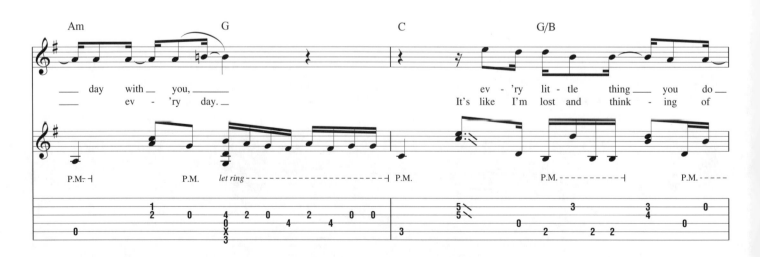

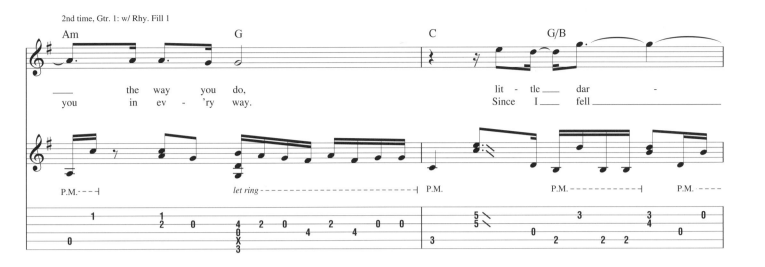

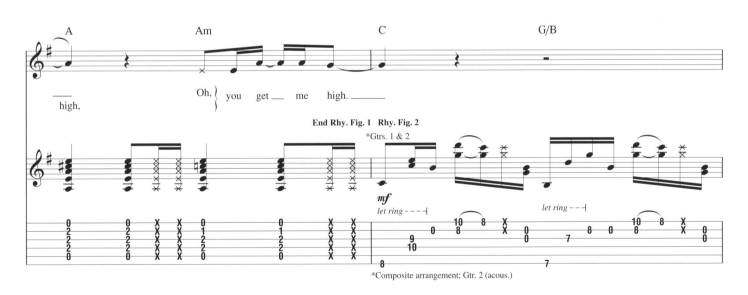

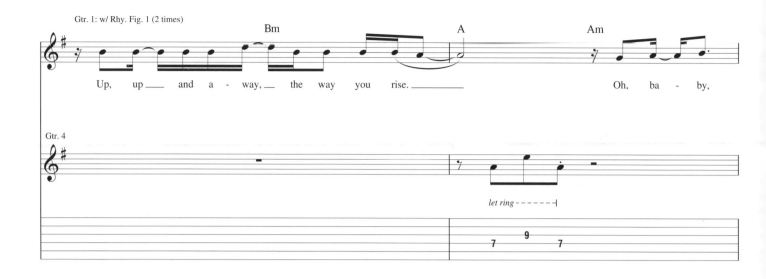

Up, up and a-way, the way you rise. Oh, ba-by,

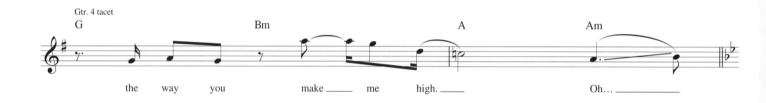

the way you make me high. Oh...

Bridge

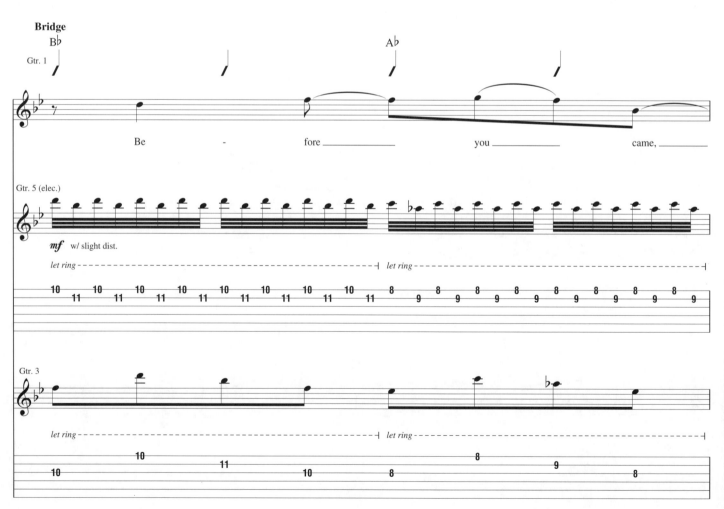

Be - fore you came,

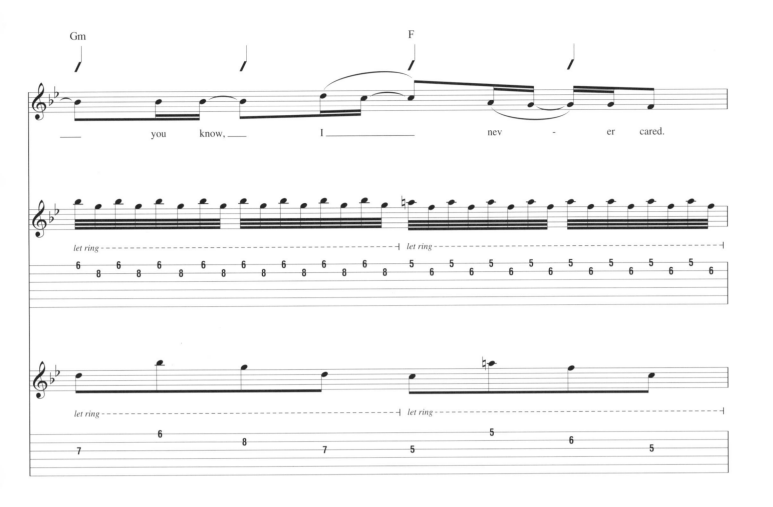

you know, ___ I _____ nev - er cared.

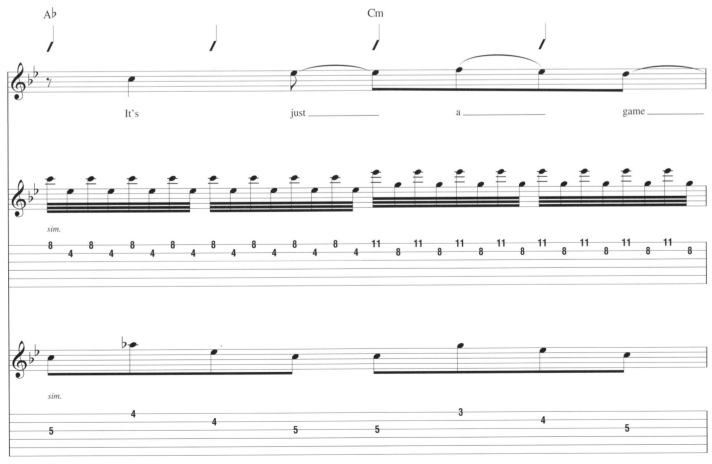

It's just _____ a _____ game _____

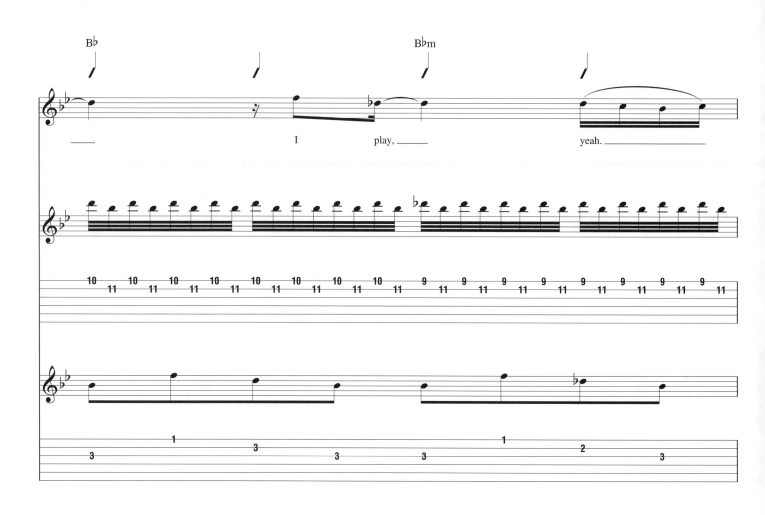

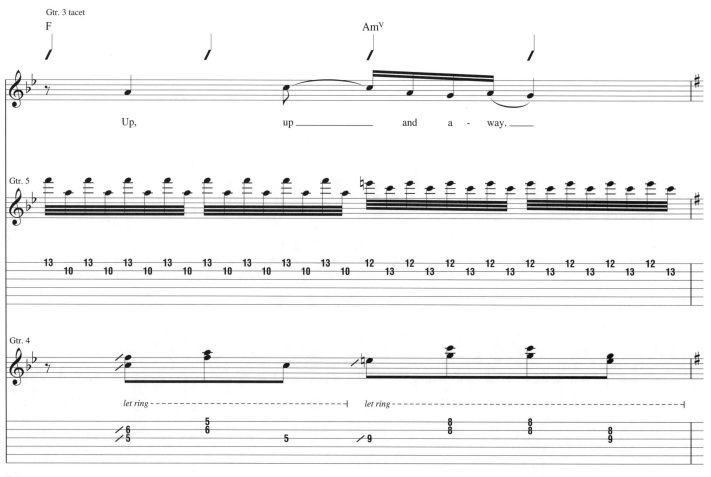

Please don't ev-er let me go. You've done noth-ing to me but up, up and a-way you go.

Gtr. 1: w/ Rhy. Fig. 3 (last 2 meas.)
Gtr. 3: w/ Riff A (last 2 meas.)

Up, up and a-way. Oh, you take me, ba-

Guitar Solo
Gtr. 1: w/ Rhy. Fig. 2 (4 times)
Gtr. 3: w/ Riff B

by, yeah, oh. Mm,

Gtr. 4
w/ slight dist.
P.M. P.M. P.M.

ba-by. Oh,

P.M. P.M. P.M. P.M.

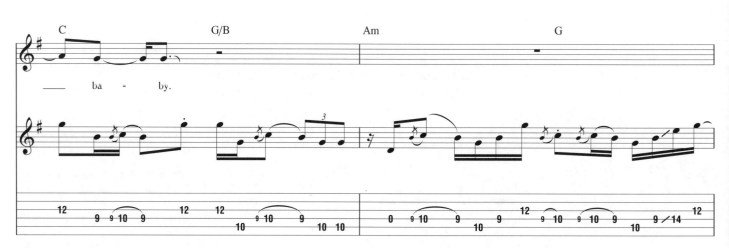

ba-by.

TOO HIGH

Words and Music by
David J. Matthews

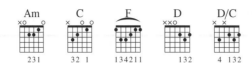

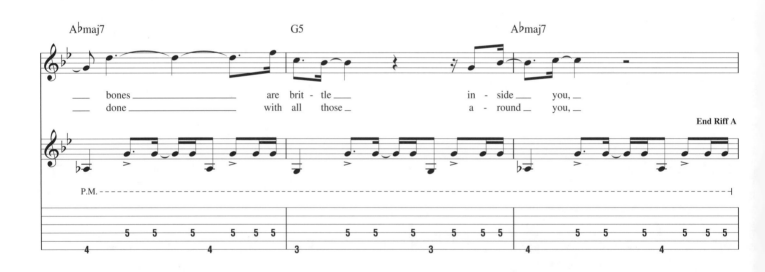

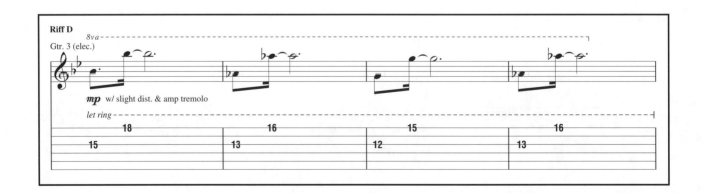

Outro

1st & 2nd times, Gtr. 3: w/ *pick harmonics

N.C.

*Fret C at 3rd string, 5th fret and play random pick harmonics.

Gtrs. 1, 2 & 4 tacet

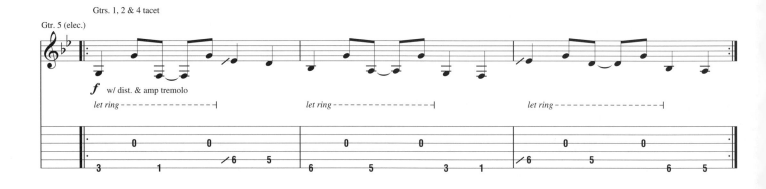

Gtr. 5 tacet

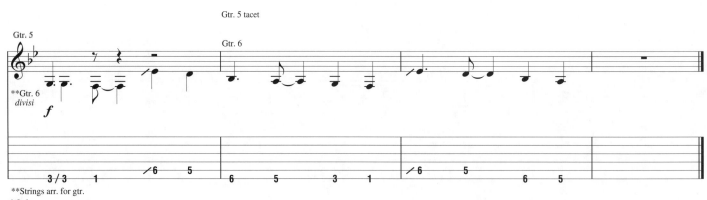

**Strings arr. for gtr.

GRAVEDIGGER (ACOUSTIC)

Words and Music by
David J. Matthews

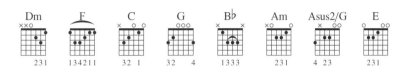

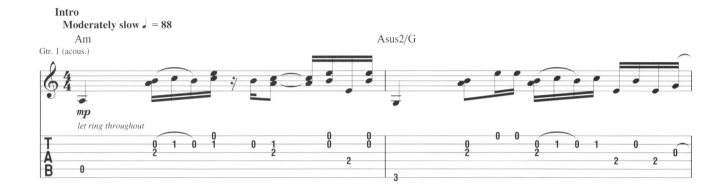

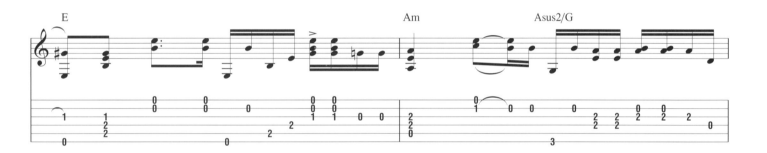

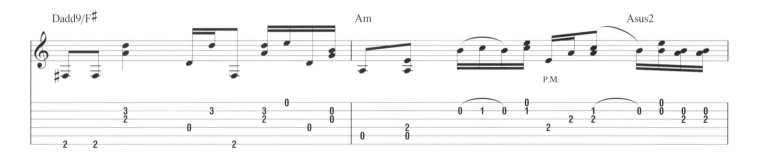

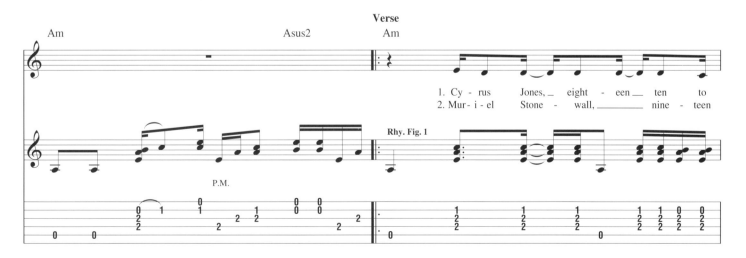

1. Cy - rus Jones, __ eight - een __ ten to
2. Mur - i - el Stone - wall, _____ nine - teen

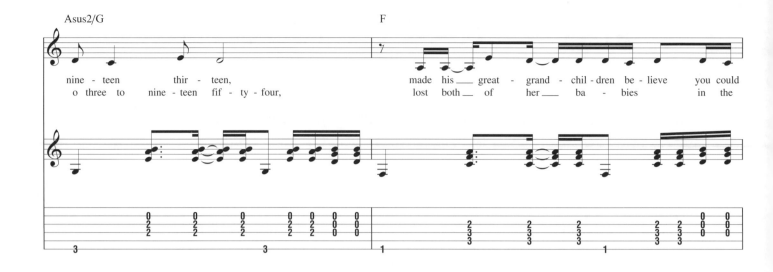

nine - teen thir - teen,
o three to nine - teen fif - ty - four,

made his ___ great - grand - chil - dren be - lieve you could
lost both ___ of her ___ ba - bies in the

Gtr. 1: w/ Rhy. Fig. 1

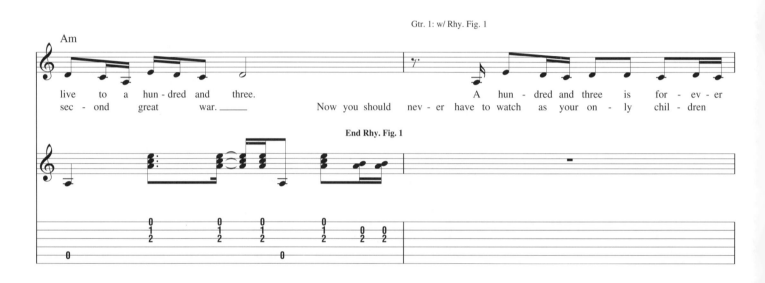

live to a hun - dred and three.
sec - ond great war. ___

A hun - dred and three is for - ev - er
Now you should nev - er have to watch as your on - ly chil - dren

End Rhy. Fig. 1

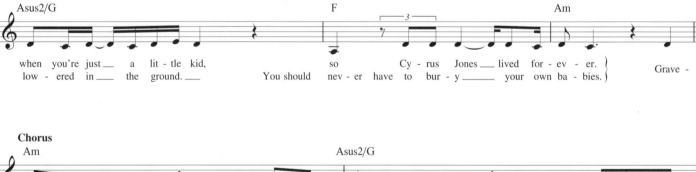

when you're just ___ a lit - tle kid,
low - ered in ___ the ground. ___

so Cy - rus Jones ___ lived for - ev - er.
You should nev - er have to bur - y ___ your own ba - bies.

Grave -

Chorus

dig - ger, ___

when you dig my grave,

could you make it shal -

Guitar Notation Legend

Guitar Music can be notated three different ways: on a *musical staff*, in *tablature*, and in *rhythm slashes*.

RHYTHM SLASHES are written above the staff. Strum chords in the rhythm indicated. Use the chord diagrams found at the top of the first page of the transcription for the appropriate chord voicings. Round noteheads indicate single notes.

THE MUSICAL STAFF shows pitches and rhythms and is divided by bar lines into measures. Pitches are named after the first seven letters of the alphabet.

TABLATURE graphically represents the guitar fingerboard. Each horizontal line represents a string, and each number represents a fret.

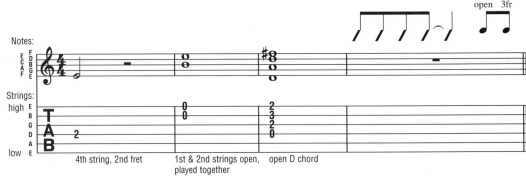

4th string, 2nd fret   1st & 2nd strings open, played together   open D chord

HALF-STEP BEND: Strike the note and bend up 1/2 step.

WHOLE-STEP BEND: Strike the note and bend up one step.

GRACE NOTE BEND: Strike the note and immediately bend up as indicated.

SLIGHT (MICROTONE) BEND: Strike the note and bend up 1/4 step.

BEND AND RELEASE: Strike the note and bend up as indicated, then release back to the original note. Only the first note is struck.

PRE-BEND: Bend the note as indicated, then strike it.

VIBRATO: The string is vibrated by rapidly bending and releasing the note with the fretting hand.

WIDE VIBRATO: The pitch is varied to a greater degree by vibrating with the fretting hand.

HAMMER-ON: Strike the first (lower) note with one finger, then sound the higher note (on the same string) with another finger by fretting it without picking.

PULL-OFF: Place both fingers on the notes to be sounded. Strike the first note and without picking, pull the finger off to sound the second (lower) note.

LEGATO SLIDE: Strike the first note and then slide the same fret-hand finger up or down to the second note. The second note is not struck.

SHIFT SLIDE: Same as legato slide, except the second note is struck.

TRILL: Very rapidly alternate between the notes indicated by continuously hammering on and pulling off.

TAPPING: Hammer ("tap") the fret indicated with the pick-hand index or middle finger and pull off to the note fretted by the fret hand.

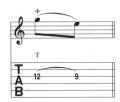

NATURAL HARMONIC: Strike the note while the fret-hand lightly touches the string directly over the fret indicated.

PINCH HARMONIC: The note is fretted normally and a harmonic is produced by adding the edge of the thumb or the tip of the index finger of the pick hand to the normal pick attack.

PICK SCRAPE: The edge of the pick is rubbed down (or up) the string, producing a scratchy sound.

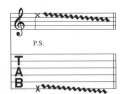

MUFFLED STRINGS: A percussive sound is produced by laying the fret hand across the string(s) without depressing, and striking them with the pick hand.

PALM MUTING: The note is partially muted by the pick hand lightly touching the string(s) just before the bridge.

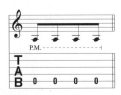

RAKE: Drag the pick across the strings indicated with a single motion.

TREMOLO PICKING: The note is picked as rapidly and continuously as possible.

VIBRATO BAR DIVE AND RETURN: The pitch of the note or chord is dropped a specified number of steps (in rhythm) then returned to the original pitch.

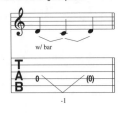

VIBRATO BAR SCOOP: Depress the bar just before striking the note, then quickly release the bar.

VIBRATO BAR DIP: Strike the note and then immediately drop a specified number of steps, then release back to the original pitch.

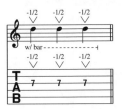

 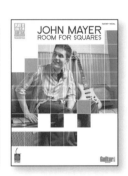

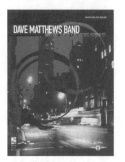